# The International Soup Book

# The International Soup Book

Edited
by
Susan R. Friedland

HarperCollins*Publishers*

# Acknowledgments

The editor and publisher are grateful to Victoria Kalish of Williams-Sonoma, who suggested that a soup book would be a good idea; to Kate Stark of HarperCollins, whose meticulous follow-through and enthusiasm was an enormous help; to Sharon Bowers, formerly of HarperCollins, who did a lot of the research for the book; to Mary Kurtz, whose copyediting skills and commitment to precision have saved many an author from embarrassment and whose work on this book focused, sharpened, and improved it; and to Joseph Rutt, whose elegant and lively design showcases the soups.

*Frontispiece: Clam Soup (recipe on page 54) and Chicken Soup (recipe on page 80). Photographs on pages 23 and 63 by Joyce Oudkerk Pool.*

FIRST EDITION

*Designed by Joseph Rutt*

Library of Congress Cataloging-in-Publication Data

The international soup book / edited by Susan R. Friedland. — 1st ed.
p. cm.
Includes index.
ISBN 0-06-757551-X
1. Soups.   2. Cookery, International.   I. Friedland, Susan R.
TX757.I58  1998
641.8'13—dc21   97-53171

98 99 00 01 02 ❖/QT 10 9 8 7 6 5 4 3 2 1

"Beautiful soup! Who cares for fish,
Game, or any other dish?
Who would not give all else for two pennyworth
only of beautiful soup?"

— LEWIS CARROLL,
    *Alice's Adventures in Wonderland*

# Contents

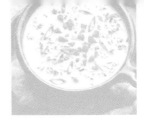

# CHAPTER 2
# Vegetables    19

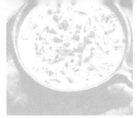

"Of soup and love,
the first is the best."

—Thomas Fuller,
*Gnomologia*

# Introduction

Of all foods, it's soup that warms the heart, fills the stomach, satisfies in all ways. Healthy, hearty, elegant, forgiving: soup is all these. And this collection, culled from "The Beautiful" series of cookbooks, offers a range from well-bred starters to a formal meal (Artichoke or Cream of Olive) to hearty main-course soups that *are* the meal (Bouillabaisse, Aromatic Braised Beef with Noodles in Rich Broth are but two).

The soups were born throughout the world. Though many carry "USA" as the country of origin, that is but another testament to the rich legacy of our immigrant heritage. Shrimp Wonton Soup with Vegetable Flowers was inspired by Chinese cooks; Seafood Gumbo by the many strains that created the fabulous Creole cuisine.

Whatever your mood, your larder, your food preferences, here are soups galore to tempt and please.

*Susan R. Friedland*

# I

# Beans
# Grains
# Legumes
# Nuts
# &
# Tubers

# Spelt Soup

*Minestra di Farro*

Serves 6

**Spelt is a kind of wheat grown mainly in Umbria, Latium, and the Abruzzi. It is used in soup either whole or roughly chopped.**

7 ounces pork rind or a ham bone

1 onion, chopped

3 ounces unsmoked bacon, chopped

1 pound plum tomatoes, put through a food mill

1 head leaf lettuce, shredded

8 cups Beef Stock (page 127)

2 tablespoons chopped fresh marjoram

1 tablespoon chopped fresh thyme

Salt

Freshly ground black pepper

3 scant cups spelt, barley, or chick-peas

Simmer the pork rind or ham bone in water to cover for about 20 minutes. Drain and cut the rind into small pieces; discard the ham bone.

Fry the onion and bacon gently in a large saucepan over low heat until the onion is translucent. Add the tomatoes, lettuce, pork rind (if using), stock, and herbs and boil for 30 minutes. Season with salt and pepper and add the spelt. Simmer for a further 20 minutes and serve.

# Lentil Soup with Fruit

*Lentejas con Fruta*

Serves 6 to 8

**In this dish, the lentils' earthy qualities are complemented by the smoky pork and sweet fruit flavors.**

2 cups dried lentils

8 cups water

8 ounces bacon, chopped

8 ounces chorizo, or other spicy sausage, casings removed and cut into chunks

1 cup chopped onion

2 cloves garlic, minced

2 slices fresh pineapple, chopped

1 plantain or large firm banana (about 12 ounces), peeled and sliced

1 teaspoon salt

1/2 teaspoon freshly ground black pepper

6 small scallions

2 tablespoons oil

4 smoked pork chops

Place the lentils and water in a large saucepan and bring to a boil. Lower the heat and simmer, covered, for 45 minutes. If you need to add more water, be sure that it is hot. Drain the lentils, reserving the cooking liquid.

In a large saucepan, sauté the bacon over medium heat for 2 minutes. Add the chorizo and cook, covered, for 3 minutes. Add the onion and garlic and sauté for 3 minutes. Add the lentils, pineapple, plantain, salt, and pepper and cook, covered, over low heat for 10 minutes. Add 2 cups of the liquid in which the lentils cooked and the scallions; cover and cook over low heat for 30 minutes.

While the mixture is cooking, heat the oil in a skillet. Add the smoked pork chops and sauté for 3 minutes on each side. Add the chops to the pan with the lentils and cook, covered, for 5 minutes.

Note: This should not be a soup, but rather a lentil casserole. If you prefer it less thick, add 1 cup water.

# Black Bean Soup

*Sopa de Frijol*

Serves 6

**The ubiquitous bean makes a filling and soothing soup. There is no substitute for the *epazote*; while it can be left out, its unique flavor will be missed. This is an easy plant to grow, and it can even be kept in a pot in the kitchen during the winter months, or used dried.**

3 cups Pot Beans

   (recipe follows)

2 to 3 cups water

4 slices bacon, chopped

⅓ cup finely chopped onion

1 small sprig *epazote*

1 tablespoon dried oregano

Salt

Oil for frying

4 day-old corn tortillas, cut into

   thin strips

6 tablespoons crème fraîche

6 slices lime

In a blender, purée the pot beans with 2 cups water.

Brown the bacon in a large saucepan without adding any oil. When the fat has cooked off, remove the bacon and set aside. Sauté the onion in the bacon fat until transparent, then add the bean purée. Cook, stirring constantly, until the mixture comes to a boil, then lower the heat and add the *epazote* and oregano. Add salt to taste and cook, covered, for 10 minutes. If the soup is too thick, add the remaining 1 cup water.

Heat ½ inch oil in a small skillet and, when hot, add the tortilla strips a few at a time. Fry, turning at least once, for about 3 minutes, or until golden brown. Remove from the oil with a slotted spatula and drain on absorbent paper. (If using fresh tortillas, dry first in a preheated 250°F oven for an hour.)

To serve, place 1 tablespoon of crème fraîche in each soup bowl and ladle the soup on top. Garnish with the tortilla strips, bacon, and a slice of lime.

# Pot Beans

*Frijoles de la Olla*

Makes 3 cups

2 cups dried black, pinto, or pink
   beans

⅓ onion

3 tablespoons lard or bacon
   drippings

1 sprig *epazote*

2 teaspoons salt

3 chiles serranos

Rinse the beans, cover with 10 cups of room-temperature water, and let soak for at least 3 hours. Discard any beans that float, then drain.

Place the beans in a large pot or dutch oven and add water, onion, and lard. Cook, covered, over medium heat for 1½ to 2 hours, or until tender. Make sure that there is always enough water to cover the beans; add more *hot* water if needed (be sure it is hot). When the beans are tender, uncover, add the *epazote*, salt, and chiles and cook, uncovered, for 20 minutes. Correct the seasonings.

# Bean Curd in Consommé

Serves 6 to 8

6 (4½-ounce) squares soft
   bean curd

3 egg whites

1 tablespoon softened lard

1½ tablespoons cornstarch

7 cups Chicken Stock (page
   126) or Vegetable Stock
   (page 128)

Salt

White pepper

1 pound fresh lettuce, Chinese
   cabbage, or other leafy
   Chinese green vegetable

Place the bean curd in a dish and mash until smooth.

Beat the egg whites well and stir into the bean curd. Add the lard and the cornstarch mixed with a little cold water, and beat the whole mixture together until thoroughly amalgamated. Pour into a lightly oiled square tin and place on a rack set over water in a wok, or in a steamer. Cover and steam for about 14 minutes until firm, then remove and leave to cool.

Cut the bean curd mixture into rectangular pieces.

Boil the stock and season with salt and pepper.

Rinse the greens thoroughly and separate the leaves; place them in the bottom of a serving bowl. Arrange the sliced bean curd on the vegetables, cover with the boiling stock, and serve at once.

# Lentil and Sausage Soup

Serves 6

**This soup is ideal during cool weather. It can be made up to 2 days ahead of serving, cooked, covered, and refrigerated. The flavor improves upon reheating.**

6 tablespoons olive oil

¾ pound mild pepperoni, cut into ½-inch dice

½ teaspoon ground coriander seed

1 large onion, finely chopped

1 large carrot, peeled and finely chopped

2 celery stalks, finely sliced

3 sprigs flat-leaf parsley, roughly chopped

¼ cup dry white wine

5 cups veal stock or Beef Stock (page 127)

1⅓ cups lentils, picked over and rinsed

Salt

Freshly ground black pepper

In a large, heavy pot over medium heat, warm 1 tablespoon of the oil. Add the pepperoni and sauté until the fat is fully rendered. Drain off and discard the fat; set the pepperoni aside.

In the same pot over medium heat, warm the remaining oil. Add the ground coriander and stir until fragrant, about 2 minutes. Add the onion and sauté until softened, about 5 minutes. Add the carrot, celery, and parsley and sauté until soft and just beginning to color, about 10 minutes.

Add the wine and cook over medium heat until reduced by half. Add the stock and lentils and cook gently, uncovered, until the lentils are tender, 30 to 35 minutes.

Return the pepperoni to the pot and heat through. Season to taste with salt and pepper, if necessary. (The sausage can be both salty and peppery, so the soup may not need additional seasoning.) Serve in warmed individual bowls.

*Celeriac Soup with Parsley Purée (page 34), left. Lentil and Sausage Soup, right.*

# King's Arms Tavern Cream of Peanut Soup

Serves 12

A South American native, the peanut plant was taken to Africa by the Portuguese to feed slaves headed for America. Peanuts were planted and used for forage across the South. But it wasn't until after the Civil War that they gained national acceptance, largely through the work of botanist George Washington Carver, of Alabama's Tuskegee Institute. In fact, peanut soup is sometimes called Tuskegee Soup. This recipe comes from the historic King's Arms Tavern in Colonial Williamsburg.

4 tablespoons salted butter

1 cup finely chopped white onion

2 celery stalks, finely chopped

1 tablespoon all-purpose flour

8 cups Chicken Stock (page 126)

1 cup smooth peanut butter

2 cups light cream, at room temperature

1 cup chopped roasted peanuts for garnish

In a large, heavy saucepan over medium-high heat, melt the butter. When it bubbles, add the onion and celery, reduce the heat to low, and cook, stirring, until softened, about 4 minutes.

Add the flour and stir to blend well. Add the chicken stock, increase the heat to medium-high, and bring to a boil, stirring constantly. Reduce the heat to medium-low and simmer, uncovered, for 15 minutes. Remove from the heat.

Strain the soup through a fine-meshed sieve into a large heatproof bowl, using the back of a wooden spoon to press the liquid from the solids. Discard the solids and return the sieved soup to the saucepan. Add the peanut butter and cream to the pan and stir.

Return the pan to low heat and heat through but do not boil. Serve at once, garnished with chopped roasted peanuts.

# Almond Soup

Serves 4

Smooth, creamy, and subtle, this soup may also be served with a handful of chopped mushrooms cooked in a little butter. To skin almonds, cover them with water and bring them to a boil. Drain well and cool for a minute, then rub off the skins between clean towels.

2 cups blanched toasted almonds

4 cups Chicken Stock (page 126)

1 onion, chopped

Salt

Freshly ground black pepper

2 tablespoons all-purpose flour

2 tablespoons butter, softened

1 cup heavy cream

2 tablespoons dry sherry

Chopped chives

Pulverize the almonds in a blender or food processor, leaving a few to garnish the soup. Place in a saucepan with the stock and onion, season lightly with salt and pepper, then cover and simmer for 20 minutes.

Pour the soup through a fine strainer to remove most of the solids, pressing firmly on them to extract all the flavor you can. Return the strained soup to the pan and stir about ½ cup of the strained almonds and onion back into it.

Blend the flour and butter together until smooth. Bring the soup back to a simmer and whisk in the flour mixture. Bring just to a boil, stirring frequently, and cook until the flour has disappeared and the soup has thickened slightly. Stir in the cream and sherry and season with additional salt and pepper, if necessary. Sprinkle each serving with chopped chives and the reserved toasted almonds.

# Pasta and Beans
*Pasta e Fagioli*

Serves 6

This dish may be made with dried store-bought or fresh homemade tagliatelle. *Pasta e fagioli* is also very good with the short pasta (such as *cannolicchi*) that is made especially for soup. The dish is delicious hot or cold.

1¼ cups dried white cannellini beans

2 bay leaves

2 whole garlic cloves

1 cup whole fresh sage leaves

5 tablespoons extra-virgin olive oil

2 ounces pancetta or rindless bacon, chopped

2 medium carrots, chopped

1 celery stalk, chopped

1 medium onion, chopped

4 garlic cloves, chopped

6 cups Chicken Stock (page 126)

1½ cups chopped tagliatelle

2 fresh rosemary sprigs, finely chopped

6 fresh thyme sprigs, finely chopped

Salt

Freshly ground black pepper

½ cup extra-virgin olive oil

Soak the beans overnight in cold water to cover generously. Drain. Place in a deep casserole and cover with fresh water by about 1 inch.

Preheat the oven to 350°F.

Add the bay leaves, whole garlic cloves, the sage, and 1 tablespoon oil to the beans. Cover and bake for 1½ hours.

Heat the remaining 4 tablespoons oil in a large saucepan over medium-high heat. Add the pancetta, carrots, celery, onion, and chopped garlic and sauté for several minutes. Pour in the broth, reduce the heat to low, and simmer for 1 hour.

Discard the sage and bay leaves from the beans. Purée half the beans and add them with their cooking liquid and the whole beans to the broth mixture. Bring to a boil. Add the tagliatelle and cook until al dente. Sprinkle in the rosemary and thyme and season with salt and pepper. Drizzle in ½ cup olive oil and serve.

*(photograph on page 16)*

# Toasted Flour Soup
*Minestra di Farina Tostata*

Serves 6

**Friuli is a very mountainous region whose inhabitants like robust dishes with strong flavors. They are particularly fond of hot, tasty soups, and their main dishes are nearly always based on bread or polenta.**

4 tablespoons butter

6 slices firm, coarse-textured bread

6 tablespoons all-purpose flour

1 medium onion, chopped

6 cups Beef Stock (page 127)

Salt

Freshly ground black pepper

Preheat the oven to 400°F.

Melt 1 tablespoon butter and brush over the slices of bread. Cut the bread into small cubes. Place on a foil-lined baking sheet and toast in the preheated oven until golden brown.

Melt the remaining butter in a large saucepan. Stir in the flour and onion and cook over moderate heat until the mixture becomes quite dark in color.

Stir in stock a little at a time and bring to a boil. Season with salt and pepper and simmer for 30 minutes.

Pour the soup into a tureen and serve, passing the croutons separately.

*Pasta and Beans (page 15), top.*
*Toasted Flour Soup, bottom.*

# 2
# Vegetables

# Vegetable Soup with Basil and Garlic

*Soupe au Pistou*

There are no exact proportions for this vegetable soup. The choice of vegetables and how much of each to use is up to you. Usually *soupe au pistou* contains carrots, green beans, shell beans, zucchini, potatoes, tomatoes, and pasta. You can even substitute ½ cup dried small navy beans (soaked overnight in water to cover, drained, and then cooked in water to cover until tender) for the fresh shell beans, adding them with the green beans.

This soup sounds like minestrone—and essentially it is. And provençal *pistou* is none other than Genoese pesto, the classic mixture of basil, garlic, and Parmesan. The word *pistou* means "pounded" in niçoise dialect, and is not too distant from *pestle,* the implement traditionally used to pound the basil and garlic to a paste. *Pistou* keeps well in the refrigerator; top it with a film of olive oil to preserve its color. Never "cook" *pistou,* as it will turn an unpleasant brown and lose its fragrance. Simply stir it into the soup or into pasta just before serving.

*(continued)*

# Vegetable Soup with Basil and Garlic

Serves 6 to 8

**For the Soup:**

3 tablespoons olive oil

4 onions, diced
   (about 6 cups)

6 carrots, peeled and sliced
   (about 2 cups)

4 celery stalks, diced
   (about 1 cup)

1 pound tomatoes, peeled,
   seeded, and diced (about
   2 cups)

8 cups water or Chicken
   Stock (page 126), or as
   needed to cover

6 new potatoes, unpeeled,
   diced (about 3 cups)

1 cup shell beans

1/2 pound green beans, cut
   into 1-inch lengths

4 zucchini, cut in half
   lengthwise and then
   sliced 1/2 inch thick

4 cups coarsely sliced Swiss
   chard (optional)

3 ounces macaroni or small
   pasta shells

Salt

Freshly ground black pepper

**For the *Pistou:***

1 teaspoon finely minced garlic

Salt

2/3 cup tightly packed fresh basil
   leaves

1/4 cup freshly grated Parmesan
   cheese

1/3 cup olive oil

Salt

Freshly ground black pepper

Extra-virgin olive oil for serving

Freshly grated Parmesan cheese
   for serving

In a large soup pot over medium heat, warm the oil. Add the onions and sauté until tender, about 10 minutes. Add the carrots and celery and sauté for a few minutes longer. Then add the tomatoes and stock and simmer, uncovered, for 10 minutes.

Add the potatoes and shell beans and simmer for 5 minutes. Then add the green beans, zucchini, Swiss chard, and pasta and continue to simmer until all the vegetables and the pasta are tender, 15 to 20 minutes longer. Season to taste with salt and pepper.

While the soup is simmering, make the *pistou*. In a mortar with a pestle, grind the garlic to a paste with a little salt. Alternatively, chop fine. Pack the basil leaves and garlic into a blender or a food processor fitted with the metal blade. Process to combine. Add the Parmesan and process to combine. Gradually add the olive oil in a thin, steady stream and process just until a coarse emulsion forms. Do not overblend; there should still be some texture. Season to taste with salt and pepper.

Remove the soup from the heat and stir in the *pistou*. Serve at once, topped with a drizzle of fruity olive oil and a sprinkling of Parmesan.

# Rivel Soup with Corn

Serves 6

**This is an old Mennonite recipe. *Rivel* literally means "lump." The rivels, or lumps, of dough are like small dumplings in the soup pot. The dumplings must be tiny, so do not overwork the dough or it will clump together in large pieces. Rich milk (or half milk and half light cream) is often used instead of chicken stock.**

⅔ cup all-purpose flour
   (approximately)

¼ teaspoon salt

1 egg, lightly beaten

8 cups Chicken Stock
   (page 126)

2 cups corn kernels, from
   4 large ears

Salt

Freshly ground black pepper

1 tablespoon chopped fresh
   chives

To make the rivels, combine the flour with the salt in a bowl. Add the egg and work gently with your fingertips until the mixture is crumbly. Add more flour if necessary.

Heat the stock to boiling in a large heavy saucepan. Reduce the heat and add the corn and bits of the rivel mixture to create small dumplings. Simmer, uncovered, for 5 minutes. Add salt and pepper to taste. Sprinkle with chives before serving.

# French Onion Soup

*Gratinée à l'Oignon*

Serves 4

**This thick, fragrant soup, invigorating and robust, is thought to have originated in Lyon.**

6 tablespoons unsalted butter

1 pound large onions, thinly sliced

1 tablespoon all-purpose flour

1½ quarts Beef Stock (page 127) or Chicken Stock (page 126)

Salt

Freshly ground black pepper

12 slices French bread

¾ cup grated Swiss cheese

Parsley sprigs (optional)

Melt the butter in a heavy 4-quart saucepan. Add the onions and cook over low heat, stirring constantly, for 20 minutes, or until they become soft and golden. Sprinkle in flour and stir for 2 minutes. Pour in the stock, season with salt and pepper, and bring to a boil. Cover and cook over very low heat for 45 minutes, stirring from time to time.

Preheat the broiler.

Toast the slices of bread on both sides under the broiler. Divide them among four flameproof soup bowls and sprinkle with the cheese. Pour the soup into the bowls and slide the bowls under the broiler, close to the heat source; broil just long enough to melt and lightly brown the cheese. Serve immediately, garnished with parsley sprigs, if desired.

# Ribollita

Serves 6

*Ribollita* **literally means "reboiled." This soup is usually made in plentiful quantities and the next day is boiled again for a few minutes, so that it ends up very thick. A little additional oil is drizzled in before serving.**

1¼ pounds kidney beans, soaked overnight in water to cover

½ cup extra-virgin olive oil

½ onion, finely chopped

1 carrot, finely chopped

1 celery stalk, finely chopped

2 garlic cloves, finely chopped

3 ounces pancetta or rindless bacon, chopped

1 pound black or Savoy cabbage, chopped

10 cups Beef Stock (page 127)

1 tablespoon fresh thyme

12 thin slices firm, coarse-textured bread

Salt

Freshly ground black pepper

Simmer the beans in fresh water just to cover over very low heat for 1½ hours. Put a little more than half of them through a sieve, or purée in a food processor.

Heat 2 tablespoons oil in a large saucepan over moderate heat. Add the onion, carrot, celery, garlic, and pancetta and cook for a few minutes. Add the cabbage and cook, stirring, for a minute or two. Add the stock and thyme and bring to a boil, then simmer, covered, over very low heat for 2 hours.

Add the bean purée and the whole beans and simmer, uncovered, for another 10 minutes. Pour the soup over the bread slices in a flameproof casserole and set aside, covered, in a cool place.

The next day, bring the soup to a boil and simmer for 2 minutes. Pour into soup bowls. Add the rest of the oil and salt and pepper to taste. Serve hot.

# Tomato and Bread Soup
*Pappa al Pomodoro*
Serves 6

**The Tuscans do not like to throw bread away. When it is stale they use it in a number of delicious dishes, such as this very tasty thick soup that is simple to make— but the bread and oil must be of the best quality.**

1 cup extra-virgin olive oil

3 garlic cloves, chopped

½ cup chopped fresh sage leaves

½ pound stale, firm, coarse-textured bread

Salt

Freshly ground black pepper

8 cups Beef Stock (page 127)

2 pounds tomatoes, peeled

Heat the oil in a saucepan over moderate heat. Add the garlic and sage leaves and cook until the garlic begins to color.

Meanwhile, slice the bread very thin. Add the slices to the oil and brown well on both sides, stirring with a wooden spoon. Season with salt and pepper.

Bring the broth to a boil in another large saucepan.

Put the tomatoes through a food mill directly into the bread mixture, or chop fine and cook for a few minutes over high heat, stirring. Pour in the boiling broth, reduce the heat, and simmer, covered, for 40 minutes. Taste and add salt if necessary.

Pour the soup into a tureen and serve.

# Garlic and Sage Soup

*Aïgo Bouido*

Serves 6

**As garlic and sage are considered beneficial to good health, this traditional soup is reputed to be a tonic.**

6 to 8 cloves garlic, finely minced

3 large or 6 small fresh sage leaves, chopped

2 fresh thyme sprigs

6 egg yolks, lightly beaten

Salt

Freshly ground black pepper

6 slices oven-toasted French bread

3 tablespoons extra-virgin olive oil

6 tablespoons freshly grated Parmesan cheese

In a 2-quart saucepan over high heat, combine the garlic, sage, thyme, and 6 cups of water and bring to a boil. Reduce the heat to low and simmer, uncovered, for 20 minutes.

Add a little hot soup to the egg yolks and slowly pour the yolk mixture back into the soup. Season to taste with salt and pepper. Place a slice of bread in each of 6 soup bowls. Cover with soup, drizzle with the olive oil, and sprinkle each serving with Parmesan.

# Bread Soup
*Sopa de Pan*
Serves 6

**This unusual and filling bread soup, with its colorful layers of fruits and vegetables, is a typical dish from San Cristóbal de las Casas, in Chiapas.**

6 cups Chicken Stock (page 126)

2 carrots, peeled and coarsely chopped

1 2-inch cinnamon stick

1 sprig thyme

1 sprig marjoram

½ teaspoon freshly ground black pepper

¼ cup dry white wine

Salt

3 cups cubed white bread, either a baguette or hard rolls

6 tablespoons unsalted butter

2 tablespoons oil

1 large onion, sliced

3 cloves garlic, minced

1½ pounds tomatoes, peeled and thickly sliced

3 hard-cooked eggs, sliced

3 teaspoons chopped capers

3 tablespoons chopped green olives (optional)

¼ cup raisins

Ground cinnamon

½ cup crumbled *queso añejo* or feta cheese (optional)

Place the chicken stock, carrots, cinnamon stick, thyme, marjoram, pepper, and wine in a saucepan. Bring to a boil, cover, and cook over medium heat for 10 minutes, or until the carrots are tender. Add salt to taste. Discard the cinnamon stick, thyme, and marjoram and set the stock aside.

Preheat the oven to 400°F. Place the bread cubes in a baking pan and bake for 10 to 15 minutes, or until lightly browned.

Heat the butter in a skillet. Add half the bread cubes and fry for a few minutes until they are golden brown. Transfer to a plate covered with absorbent paper. Repeat the procedure with the rest of the bread cubes. Set aside.

Heat the oil in a skillet, add the onion and garlic, and sauté for 3 minutes. Add the tomatoes and cook over medium heat, stirring constantly, for 10 minutes. Set aside.

Fifteen minutes before serving, preheat the oven to 425°F. Bring the chicken stock to a simmer. Divide the bread cubes and stewed tomatoes among 6 ovenproof bowls, garnish each with 2 slices of egg, and add the hot chicken stock. Sprinkle with capers, olives, raisins, and a pinch of cinnamon. Bake until the soup starts to boil. Serve hot, sprinkled with the *queso añejo* if desired.

# Tortilla Soup

*Sopa de Tortilla*

Serves 6

**If just one soup could be labeled the classic Mexican soup, it would probably be this one, combining as it does the traditional flavors and textures of the country's chiles, tomato, avocado, *epazote*, and tortilla.**

3 garlic cloves

½ onion, cut into chunks

3 ripe tomatoes

6 cups Chicken Stock
(page 126)

1 tablespoon oil

2 small sprigs *epazote*

Salt

Freshly ground black pepper

8 to 10 day-old corn tortillas

Oil for frying

2 to 3 chiles pasillas

2 avocados, peeled, pitted, and
sliced or chopped

1¼ cups crumbled *queso fresco*
or feta cheese

½ cup heavy cream or crème
fraîche

3 limes, halved

Roast the garlic, onion, and tomatoes (see note). Peel and core the tomatoes and purée in a blender with the garlic and onion, adding ¼ cup of the chicken stock if necessary.

Heat 1 tablespoon oil in a large saucepan over high heat and sauté the tomato purée. Boil for 2 minutes, lower the heat, and cook, stirring constantly, for another 5 minutes or until the purée thickens and changes color.

Add the remaining chicken stock and *epazote*. Return to a boil, add salt and pepper to taste, and cook, covered, over medium heat for 15 minutes.

Cut the tortillas in half and cut each half into thin strips. Heat ½ inch of oil in a small skillet and, when hot, add the tortilla pieces a few at a time and fry, turning at least once, for about 3 minutes, or until golden brown. Remove from the oil with a slotted spatula and drain on absorbent paper. (If using fresh tortillas, dry first in a preheated 250°F oven for 1 hour.)

Cut the chiles into ½-inch rings and remove their seeds. Fry in the hot oil for about 1 minute until crisp. Drain and set aside.

Five minutes before serving, reheat the soup and add the fried tortilla strips. Garnish each

bowl of soup with a few chile rings and some of the avocado. Sprinkle with the cheese. Pass the cream, lime halves, and the remaining chile rings and avocado in separate bowls so that each person can add them to taste.

Note: Roast the peeled garlic and onion and the unpeeled tomatoes on a griddle over medium-high heat until charred, turning as needed.

# Celeriac Soup with Parsley Purée

Serves 8 to 10

**Celeriac (celery root) has a fairly short season beginning in autumn and lasting into winter. This recipe is from Robin Howard, the chef and owner of a restaurant in Goulburn.**

**For the Soup:**

2 tablespoons unsalted butter

4 celery roots (about 1½ pounds total weight) peeled and diced

1 tart apple, peeled, cored, and diced

6 cups Chicken Stock (page 126)

Salt

Freshly ground black pepper

**For the Parsley Purée:**

1 bunch flat-leaf parsley, stems removed

⅔ cup pine nuts, lightly toasted

Salt

Freshly ground black pepper

1 cup olive oil

To make the soup, melt the butter in a heavy pot over medium-low heat. Add the celery roots and cook, stirring occasionally, until golden, about 20 minutes. Add the apple and cook, stirring, until the apple is tender, another 10 minutes. Stir in the stock. Pass the soup through a fine-mesh sieve or a food mill fitted with the coarse blade. Return the soup to the pot, season to taste with salt and pepper, and reheat.

To make the parsley purée, in a food processor fitted with the metal blade, place the parsley, pine nuts, and salt and pepper to taste. Process until smooth. With the processor running, gradually pour in the olive oil; the mixture should be thick.

To serve, spoon 1 tablespoon of the parsley purée into each warmed soup bowl. Ladle the soup into the bowls and serve immediately.

*(photograph on page 10)*

# "Cappuccino" of Cauliflower and Parsley

Serves 4

**The charm of this easy and inexpensive soup from Fabrice Boone is its lightness. The trick is to blend and aerate it as close to serving time as possible. It will have a more pronounced flavor if made 1 or 2 days ahead. Reheat the soup and spoon on the parsley purée at the very last moment.**

3 tablespoons olive oil

⅓ cup finely chopped celery

⅓ cup finely chopped onion

⅓ cup finely chopped leek

3 cups Chicken Stock
    (page 126)

2½ cups finely chopped
    cauliflower

¾ cup heavy cream

1 bunch curly parsley, coarsely
    chopped

In a heavy pot over medium heat, warm the oil. Add the celery, onion, and leek and sauté until softened, about 5 minutes. Add the chicken stock and cauliflower and bring to a boil. Reduce the heat to medium and simmer until the cauliflower is tender, 5 to 10 minutes.

Working in batches, transfer to a blender and purée until smooth. Return the soup to a clean pot and add half of the cream. Reheat to serving temperature; keep warm.

Rinse out the blender container and add the parsley to it. Blend to chop fine. Add the remaining cream and blend until well mixed and frothy. If the mixture needs more liquid, add a tablespoonful of the cauliflower soup and blend until smooth. Transfer the purée to a small pan and bring to a boil. Remove from the heat.

Ladle the cauliflower soup into warmed individual bowls. Spoon the parsley mixture onto the hot soup. Serve at once.

# Artichoke Soup

Serves 6 to 8

A delicate and elegant soup to serve hot or cold, and a good way to begin a fancy dinner. It is worth starting with fresh artichokes and cooking and trimming their bottoms. There is no shortcut for this job, but you have a delicious soup as a dividend.

**For the Artichoke Preparation:**

⅔ cup all-purpose flour

½ cup lemon juice

1 teaspoon salt

8 large artichokes

**For the Soup:**

4 tablespooons butter

1 medium onion, chopped

2 celery stalks, chopped

1 garlic clove, minced

3 tablespoons all-purpose flour

4 cups Chicken Stock (page 126)

1 cup half-and-half or heavy cream

Salt

Freshly ground black pepper

2 tablespoons lemon juice

1 tablespoon chopped fresh tarragon or parsley

Lemon zest, in thin strips

Prepare the artichokes: Place the flour in a large, nonaluminum saucepan and slowly whisk in 6 cups of water; add the lemon juice and salt. Set over medium heat and bring to a boil, stirring frequently. Watch carefully, and do not let the mixture boil over. When it boils, turn the heat to low.

In the meantime, trim the artichokes. Pull off the tough outer leaves; then, with a small sharp knife, cut away and discard the remaining inner leaves to expose the thistlelike choke in the center. Trim the artichoke bottoms so that they are reasonably neat and, as you are done, drop each one into the simmering liquid. Cover the pan partially and cook for about 35 to 45 minutes, or until the artichokes are tender when pierced.

Let them cool for about an hour in the cooking liquid, then rinse them under cold water. Scrape out and discard the chokes. Refrigerate the bottoms, covered, until you are ready for them.

Purée the artichoke bottoms in a food processor or pass them through a food mill. You will have about 1⅓ cups of purée. Set aside.

To make the soup, melt the butter in a large saucepan, add the onion, celery, and garlic, and cook gently for about 10 minutes. Add the flour and cook, stirring, for about 2 minutes, then

whisk in the stock. Bring just to a boil, stirring frequently, then blend in the artichoke purée. Add the half-and-half or cream and season with salt and pepper to taste. Stir in the lemon juice.

Garnish with tarragon or parsley and strips of lemon zest. Serve hot, or chill thoroughly and serve cold.

# Cream of Olive Soup

Serves 4

**Olives come in many types in California. Chopped plain ripe black olives make a fine soup that will surprise you not only with its taste but also with its simplicity. It has a fine smoky flavor.**

3 tablespoons butter

3 tablespoons all-purpose flour

4 cups Chicken Stock
   (page 126)

Freshly ground black pepper

1 cup minced ripe black olives

1 cup heavy cream

Salt, if needed

¼ cup sherry

1 large scallion, minced

Melt the butter in a large saucepan, blend in the flour, and cook over moderate heat, stirring, for about 2 minutes. Whisk in the stock, bring to a simmer, and season generously with pepper. Stir in the olives and cream and bring the mixture back to a simmer. Taste, and add salt if necessary. Stir in the sherry and scallion and serve.

# Spiced Onion and Ale Soup

Serves 6 to 8

**Dark ale gives this hearty soup a sweet richness. Serve it in front of the fire on a damp winter evening. Try it with garlic croutons, a sprinkling of sharp Cheddar melted on top, and, of course, a hearty ale to wash it down.**

2 tablespoons butter

4 onions, cut into thin slices

1 cup diced smoked ham

3 tablespoons minced garlic

¼ teaspoon ground allspice

1 tablespoon chopped fresh
   thyme, or 1 teaspoon dried
   thyme

¼ cup Dijon mustard

1½ cups pale ale

8 cups Chicken Stock
   (page 126)

2 tablespoons cornstarch mixed
   with ½ cup cold water

Salt

Freshly ground black pepper

2 cups grated sharp Cheddar
   cheese

½ cup sliced scallions

In a large, heavy saucepan or Dutch oven, melt the butter over medium heat and cook the onions, ham, garlic, allspice, and thyme, stirring frequently, until the onions are evenly caramelized, 10 to 15 minutes.

Add the mustard, ale, and chicken stock and simmer for 15 to 20 minutes. Whisk in the cornstarch and water mixture and boil gently for 4 to 5 minutes to thicken. Reduce the heat to a low simmer and add salt and pepper.

Serve sprinkled with grated Cheddar and scallions.

# Spicy Squash Bisque with Root Vegetables

Serves 4 to 6

**For a hearty main-course meal, add slices of smoked sausage to the bisque, and accompany with a substantial salad and hot corn muffins.**

**For the Squash Bowls:**

4 to 6 orange winter squashes, about 5 to 6 inches in diameter

**For the Soup:**

¼ cup olive oil

1½ cups diced onion

4 cups peeled, cubed sweet winter squash and/or pumpkin

2 garlic cloves, minced

1½ teaspoons ground cumin

1 teaspoon crushed coriander seed

¼ teaspoon grated nutmeg

1 teaspoon cardamom pods, crushed

¼ teaspoon cayenne

1 bay leaf

1½ teaspoons salt, or to taste

3½ cups rich Chicken Stock (page 126)

¾ cup sour cream

⅓ cup corn kernels

½ cup julienned carrot

⅓ cup julienned parsnip

⅓ cup thin-diagonal-cut celery

1 small leek, white part only, thinly sliced into rounds

2 scallions, thinly sliced on the diagonal

Preheat the oven to 350°F.

To prepare the squash bowls: Cut the top third off the squash. Scoop out the seeds and loose fiber thoroughly. Place the lids back on the squash. Place the squash on a baking sheet and bake for 30 minutes, or until the flesh is tender. Set aside.

To make the soup: In a large, heavy saucepan, heat 2 tablespoons olive oil over medium-high heat; add the onion and sauté for 2 to 3 minutes. Add the cubed squash, garlic, spices, and seasonings. Sauté for another 2 to 3 minutes. Add the chicken stock and bring to a boil. Turn down the heat, partially cover the pan, and simmer for approximately 15 to 18 minutes, or until the squash is very tender.

Remove from the heat; remove and discard the bay leaf. In a blender or food processor, carefully purée the hot soup in small batches with the sour cream. Pour the processed soup back in the pot and keep warm.

To serve the soup: In a large skillet, place the remaining 2 tablespoons of olive oil and heat over medium-high heat. Toss in the corn, carrot, parsnip, celery, and leek and sauté quickly until tender, about 2 to 3 minutes.

Divide the soup among the warm cooked
squash bowls or the soup bowls, and mound a
few vegetables in the center of each serving.
Garnish with scallions.

# Spring Asparagus Soup

Serves 6

**This light, creamy asparagus soup is easy to prepare yet elegant enough for a special luncheon; or serve it with country baked ham and fresh biscuits for a springtime Sunday dinner.**

2 pounds trimmed fresh
   asparagus

¼ cup olive oil

1 cup diced onions

½ cup diced shallots

1½ cups peeled and diced
   russet potatoes

5 to 6 cups Chicken Stock
   (page 126)

About 1 cup heavy cream

Salt

Freshly ground white pepper

Remove the tips from half of the asparagus, reserving the stalks. Blanch the tips in boiling water until bright green, about 30 seconds. Remove the asparagus from the water and plunge them into cold water, drain, and set aside. Cut the remaining asparagus and reserved stalks into pieces.

Heat the olive oil in a large saucepan, add the onions and shallots, and cook over moderate heat until the onions are translucent, about 5 to 7 minutes. Add the potatoes and unblanched asparagus and cook until the asparagus turns bright green. Add the chicken stock and bring just to a boil. Reduce the heat and simmer for 20 minutes, or until the potatoes and asparagus are tender.

Purée the soup in batches in a food processor until smooth. Return the soup to the saucepan and heat to steaming. Add cream to the desired thickness and heat thoroughly; do *not* boil. Add salt and pepper to taste.

Garnish with asparagus tips to serve.

# Corn Chowder

Serves 4 to 6

**The Iroquois Indians tell the tale of a mysterious spirit that came down to earth to walk on their lands. Wherever she trod, corn sprouted forth, just as corn chowders sprout forth to this day.**

6 ears of corn

6 bacon strips

1 small onion, finely chopped

1 small green pepper, seeded and finely chopped

1 red cayenne pepper or hot red chile pepper, seeded, deveined, and finely chopped

1 small celery stalk, finely chopped

3 tomatoes, peeled, seeded, and finely chopped

1 teaspoon salt

1 teaspoon sugar

⅛ teaspoon ground allspice

1 small bay leaf

2 potatoes, peeled and diced

3 cups light cream or half-and-half, at room temperature

Freshly ground black pepper

Cut the kernels from the corn, but only to half their depth. Then, with the back of the knife, scrape the cobs up and down over a rimmed plate to remove all the "milk." Set aside. The mixture will resemble scrambled eggs.

Sauté the bacon in a large heavy pot or dutch oven until crisp. Drain on paper towels. Crumble and reserve.

Discard all but 3 tablespoons bacon drippings from the pot. Add the onion and cook over medium heat until golden, 4 to 5 minutes. Add the peppers and celery and cook 2 minutes longer. Add the tomatoes, scraping the bottom and sides of the pot. Add the salt, sugar, allspice, bay leaf, potatoes, corn kernels, and corn milk. Cook over medium heat until the mixture begins to sizzle. Reduce the heat to low and cook, covered, for 30 minutes, stirring occasionally. Remove the bay leaf.

Stir the cream into the chowder and heat just to boiling. Remove from the heat and add pepper and the bacon.

# Cheese Soup

*Sopa de Queso*
Serves 8

**In some parts of Sonora, Mexico, potato chunks are added to this typical regional soup.**

1 chile poblano

1 green pepper

3 tablespoons butter

½ cup chopped onion

5 cups Chicken Stock (page 126)

2 tablespoons all-purpose flour

2 tablespoons cornstarch

¾ cup water

4 cups evaporated milk

1 teaspoon salt

1 teaspoon freshly ground black pepper

4 ounces *queso Chihuahua* (or Monterey Jack or medium-sharp Cheddar cheese), finely chopped (about 1 cup)

1 cup chopped tomato

Remove the stems, seeds, and membranes from the *chile* and pepper and cut into small dice; there should be about 1¼ cups.

Melt 1 tablespoon butter in a skillet, add the onion, and sauté for 2 minutes, or until transparent. Add the chile and pepper and cook for 3 minutes. Set aside.

Bring the stock to a boil in a large saucepan. Stir the flour and cornstarch into the water, add to the stock, and continue to stir constantly for 2 minutes. Add the milk and lower the heat. When the stock comes to a boil, add the pepper and *chile* and cook over low heat for 5 minutes. Add the salt and pepper and cook 2 minutes more. Add the remaining 2 tablespoons butter and set aside.

Before serving, heat the soup and place 2 tablespoons of cheese and 2 tablespoons of tomato in the bottom of each bowl. Pour the hot soup on top.

# Zucchini Soup with Oatmeal

*Sopa de Calabacita con Avena*

Serves 6

**This soup was created by Adelfa Silva, a transplanted Oaxacan who for two decades has cooked in Acapulco. It combines squash with oatmeal to produce a thick soup.**

2 tablespoons butter

1 tablespoon minced onion

1 ¼ pounds small zucchini, chopped

½ cup quick-cooking oatmeal

6 cups milk

Salt

Freshly ground black pepper

Melt the butter in a large saucepan, add the onion, and sauté for 2 minutes or until transparent. Add the zucchini and sauté for 4 minutes. Add the oatmeal and cook, stirring, for 2 minutes. Add the milk a little at a time, stirring constantly. Add salt and pepper to taste. Cook, covered, over low heat for 15 minutes or until the zucchini are tender.

*(photograph on page 50)*

# Chile and Cheese Soup
*Minguichi*
Serves 6

**This unusual soup is named for the Purépecha (Tarascan) Indian combination of chiles and *queso cotija*, the local cheese of the region. Here, *manchego* is substituted; Muenster also gives a good but different flavor.**

1½ pounds tomatoes, quartered

1 tablespoon oil

½ tablespoon butter

½ cup finely chopped onion

1 garlic clove, finely chopped

Kernels from 5 ears young corn

1½ teaspoons salt

½ teaspoon freshly ground
   black pepper

3 cups Chicken Stock
   (page 126)

2 chiles poblanos, roasted,
   peeled, membranes
   removed, and cut into strips

1 cup milk

1½ cups diced *manchego,*
   Muenster, or young pecorino
   cheese

In a blender, purée the tomatoes, strain, and set aside.

Heat the oil and butter in a deep skillet, add the onion, garlic, and corn, and sauté for 5 minutes.

Add the puréed tomatoes, salt, and pepper, and simmer, uncovered, for 5 minutes. Stir in the stock and simmer for 10 minutes. Add the chile strips and cook for 5 minutes. Add the milk and simmer for 5 more minutes.

Before serving, divide the cheese among 6 soup bowls. Pour the hot soup over and serve.

*Zucchini Soup with Oatmeal (top).*
*Chile and Cheese Soup (bottom).*

# 3
# Fish

# Clam Soup

*Sopa de Almejas*
Serves 6

**This soup is usually made with the sweet pismo clams of Ensenada, but any other fresh clams can be used instead of canned.**

3 tablespoons olive oil

¾ cup chopped onion

2 cups chopped celery

1 garlic clove, minced

3 cups peeled and cubed
   potatoes

8 cups Chicken Stock
   (page 126)

Salt

4 pounds fresh clams, steamed,
   opened, and chopped, or
   2 cans (2 pounds) chopped
   clams, drained, with juice
   reserved

1½ cups finely chopped parsley

Juice of 1 lime

Heat 1 tablespoon oil in a large pot or dutch oven, add the onion, celery, and garlic and cook for 5 minutes or until transparent.

Add the potatoes, chicken stock, and 1 cup of the clam juice and simmer, covered, over low heat for 15 minutes or until the potatoes are tender. Add salt to taste.

Ten minutes before serving, bring the mixture to a boil and add the chopped clams. Return to a boil and add the chopped parsley, the remaining olive oil, and lime juice. Serve immediately.

# Rice Soup with Shrimp
*Khao Tom Goong*

Serves 4

**Rice soups are easy to prepare. Cooked rice is usually used, although uncooked rice will produce the same result, only over longer time. The use of different types of shellfish or fish can provide endless variations of this flavorful dish.**

2 cups water

2 celery stalks, chopped

¼ teaspoon white pepper

1 tablespoon Maggi seasoning

½ pound fresh shrimp, shelled, deveined, and butterflied

1 cup steamed rice

2 tablespoons *nam pla* (fish sauce)

2 tablespoons oil

1 teaspoon thinly sliced garlic cloves

Cilantro leaves, for garnish

Heat the water to boiling in a large saucepan and add the chopped celery, white pepper, and Maggi seasoning.

Add the shrimp, rice, and fish sauce.

Heat to boiling and cook for 3 minutes, or until the shrimp are just cooked.

Heat the oil in a small skillet and sauté the garlic until golden brown.

Serve the soup with the fried garlic sprinkled over it, and garnish with cilantro leaves.

# Crispy Fish Spicy Soup
*Tom Yam Pla Grob*
Serves 4

**In earlier times, catfish were brought in from Cambodia. Today the grilled crispy fish are sold in markets throughout Thailand.**

½ pound fish fillets

Vegetable oil for deep-frying

4 thin slices *galangal* (see Notes)

4 shallots

4 dried jalapeño peppers

2 garlic cloves

2 stalks lemongrass, halved

⅓ cup *nam pla* (fish sauce)

½ cup tamarind juice (see Notes)

Dry the fish fillets and deep-fry them in the hot oil. Drain on paper towels, then break the fish into 2-inch pieces.

Place the *galangal*, shallots, jalapeños, garlic, and lemongrass on a charcoal grill and broil until they are slightly burned. Allow to cool, then crush, using a mortar and pestle.

Heat 3 cups of water to boiling in a large saucepan. Add the crushed vegetables, the fish pieces, fish sauce, and tamarind juice and simmer for 20 minutes. Serve at once.

Notes: *Galangal,* available in some oriental markets, is similar to fresh gingerroot, but with a pinker hue. It should be peeled before slicing.

Tamarind juice adds a sharp, sour flavor without the tartness of lemon. It can be prepared at home or can be bought in bottles in Asian food stores. Lemon or lime can act as a substitute, but the delicate flavor is lost.

To make tamarind juice, add 1 tablespoon of tamarind paste to ½ cup of hot water and stir.

# Fish and Onion Stew

*Pochouse*

Serves 6

4 pounds river fish (eel, carp, perch, pike)

5 ounces lightly salted pork fatback

5 tablespoons butter

25 tiny pickling onions, peeled

Salt

Freshly ground black pepper

3 cups white Burgundy

6 garlic cloves, peeled

¼ cup all-purpose flour

Croutons

Ask the fishmonger to scale and gut the fish and remove the heads. Cut the fish into 1½-inch chunks, rinse, and pat dry.

Rinse the fatback. Remove the rind and cut the fat into fine matchsticks. Blanch for 1 minute in boiling water, then drain, rinse, and drain again.

Melt 3 tablespoons butter in a 6-quart pot. Add the onions and fatback and cook, stirring, over low heat for 5 minutes or until lightly golden. Season lightly with salt and pepper. Pour in the wine and bring to a simmer. Add the garlic and fish and simmer for 20 minutes. Remove the fish and keep warm in a tureen. Discard the garlic.

Combine the flour and the remaining butter in a small bowl to form a soft ball. Blend in 3 tablespoons of the broth, then return the mixture to the pot and cook over low heat, stirring, for 5 minutes, or until the sauce thickens to a creamy consistency. Pour over the fish and serve immediately, accompanied by croutons.

# Bouillabaisse

**Bouillabaisse was devised by Mediterranean fishermen who, when they returned from a fishing trip, would cook their more modest fish with a few shellfish in a huge cauldron over a wood fire using olive oil, a piece of dried orange peel, and some saffron.**

**Gradually it became a highlight of the cuisine of the Midi region, each cook adding his or her own individual touch. The common factor in all the recipes is the use of as many white-fleshed fish as possible, to which may be added small crabs, mussels, and cuttlefish with their ink.**

*(continued)*

# Bouillabaisse

Serves 6 to 8

6 pounds of a mixture of fish
  and crustaceans (cod, John
  Dory, monkfish, eel, sea bass,
  snapper, red mullet,
  cuttlefish, sole, brill, small
  crabs, lobster, crayfish)

¼ cup extra-virgin olive oil

1 pound ripe tomatoes, coarsely
  chopped

2 medium carrots, peeled and
  thinly sliced

1 leek, well washed and thinly
  sliced

1 celery stalk, thinly sliced

1 onion, thinly sliced

1 sprig dried thyme

1 sprig dried rosemary

1 sprig dried fennel

1 bay leaf

1 strip dried orange peel

10 garlic cloves, peeled

10 sprigs parsley

6 pinches saffron threads

Salt

Freshly ground black pepper

2 cups dry white wine

Slices of toasted French
  bread rubbed with
  halved garlic cloves

Ask the fishmonger to scale and gut the fish and remove the heads. Reserve the heads, bones, and shells. Cut the largest fish into 1½-inch chunks and leave the others whole. Wash all the fish and pat dry. If crayfish or lobster is included, cut it in half to separate the head from the tail and remove the grainy sac from the head. Clean the cuttlefish, keeping only the body and tentacles; wash and pat dry.

Heat the oil in a 6-quart saucepan. Add the heads, bones, and shells of the fish and crustaceans and cook over low heat, stirring, for 5 minutes. Add the tomatoes, carrots, leek, celery, and onion and cook, stirring, for 5 minutes, or until the vegetables are lightly colored. Add the thyme, rosemary, fennel, bay leaf, orange peel, garlic, parsley, saffron, salt, and pepper and stir for 1 minute. Add the wine and simmer gently for 45 minutes.

Remove the fish trimmings. Purée the tomato mixture in a blender or food processor until smooth.

Wipe the saucepan and return the puréed mixture to it. Bring to a boil over low heat. Add the fish, beginning with those with the firmest flesh (cuttlefish, eel, monkfish, cod, red mullet) and later adding those with softer flesh (John Dory, sea bass, sole, brill, snapper), letting the mixture return to a simmer between additions. Finally add the crustaceans. Simmer for 10 minutes, then remove the seafood with a slotted spoon and arrange on a plate. Keep warm.

Pour the soup into a tureen and serve hot over slices of bread rubbed with garlic. Follow with the seafood as a separate course.

# Crab Hot Pot

*Kani Chiri*

Serves 4 to 6

1 fresh crab, about 3 pounds

4 squares soft bean curd

½ pound leafy green vegetables
such as spinach, mustard
greens, or Chinese cabbage

1 medium carrot

6 dried shiitake mushrooms,
soaked in warm water for
25 minutes

12 cultivated mushrooms

6 scallions

6 cups *dashi* or Fish Stock (page
129)

**For the Sauces and Dips:**

6-inch piece *daikon* (giant white
radish)

1 fresh red chile

1 large white onion

1 teaspoon salt

¾ cup lemon or lime juice

¾ cup *dashi* or Fish Stock (page
129)

½ cup light soy sauce

Cut the crab in half. Remove the undershell and discard; scrape out the inedible parts of the crab. Rinse the crab quickly in cold water; cut into small pieces, each with a leg or claw attached. Cut lengthwise along each leg with a sharp cleaver; crack the claws with the back of the cleaver.

Holding the bean curd in the palm of your hand, carefully cut into slices, then slide onto a plate. Wash the greens carefully in cold water, drain, and chop coarsely.

Peel the carrot and cut lengthwise into a five-sided shape. Make a lengthwise groove in the center of each flat side, then carefully pare away the remaining points, to give five rounded petal shapes. Cut into thin slices to make "plum blossoms." Drain the shiitake mushrooms, discard stems, and cut a deep cross into each cap. Slice the cultivated mushrooms. Trim the scallions and slice diagonally into 1½-inch lengths.

Bring the *dashi* to the boil in a flameproof earthenware pot. Add the vegetables and simmer for 3 to 4 minutes, then add the crab and simmer 3 to 4 minutes more before carefully sliding in the bean curd.

Prepare the sauces and dips as follows and serve in small dishes. Peel the *daikon*; seed the chile. Insert a chopstick into the end of the radish to form a cavity. Push the chile into the cavity, then grate them together into a paste.

Mince the onion and mix with the salt.

Mix the lemon juice, *dashi*, and soy sauce in a small saucepan and bring almost to the boil, then allow to cool.

The hot pot should be placed on a small portable cooker on the tabletop, where it can continue to simmer gently while each diner helps himself.

# Granville Island Chowder

Serves 6 to 8

**Vancouver's Granville Island Public Market opened for business in July 1979. Since then, locals and tourists have been lured by the splendid array of Pacific seafoods and succulent meats, exotic fruits and vegetables, and an endless variety of other foods and even flowers. Vancouverites cook many different versions of this chowder, depending on which fish and shellfish are available from the fishmonger at the market.**

6 bacon strips

1 onion, chopped

3 garlic cloves, minced

1 green pepper, thinly sliced

2 carrots, thinly sliced

2 tablespoons chopped fresh parsley

4 cups peeled, seeded, and coarsely chopped fresh or canned tomatoes

3 cups bottled clam juice

1½ cups dry red wine

1 tablespoon fresh thyme, or 1½ teaspoons dried thyme

Salt

Freshly ground black pepper

2 cups diced peeled potatoes

2 pounds mixed fresh shellfish and boneless fish such as peeled large shrimp, scallops, crabmeat, salmon, and snapper or other firm, white-fleshed fish fillets, cut into pieces

Oven-toasted garlic croutons

Cut the bacon into 1-inch pieces. Fry until crisp in a heavy pot or dutch oven. Add the onion, garlic, green pepper, carrots, and parsley and cook over medium heat for 10 minutes, stirring occasionally.

Add the tomatoes, clam juice, red wine, thyme, salt, and pepper, and bring to a boil for 1 minute. Lower the heat, cover the pan, and simmer for 20 minutes. Add the potatoes, cover, and simmer for 30 minutes, or until the potatoes are tender.

Add the shellfish and fish and cook, stirring gently, just until the fish turns opaque, about 5 minutes. Serve immediately, placing croutons in each serving.

# Shrimp Wonton Soup with Vegetable Flowers

Serves 4 as a light entrée, 8 as a starter

**A light, satisfying soup with the fanciful touch of vegetable flowers. Chopped chicken, pork, or crab may be substituted for the shrimp.**

**For the Wontons:**

6 ounces raw shrimp meat

1 teaspoon soy sauce

1 teaspoon minced fresh
    ginger

¼ teaspoon salt

1 tablespoon egg white

1 garlic clove, minced

2 tablespoons minced
    scallion

2 tablespoons minced red
    pepper

16 wonton skins

**For the Soup:**

4 scallions

8 cups Chicken Stock (page
    126)

1 tablespoon soy sauce

1 tablespoon slivered fresh
    ginger

2 Chinese *lop chong* sausages,
    thinly sliced (optional)

Wontons

4 large shrimp, sliced in half
    lengthwise

2-inch piece zucchini, sliced into
    8 flowers (see Note)

2-inch piece yellow summer
    squash, sliced into 8 flowers
    (see Note)

2-inch piece carrot, sliced into 8
    flowers (see Note)

2 fresh shiitake mushrooms,
    thinly sliced, about ½ cup
    (optional)

4 fresh cilantro sprigs

4 stalks of enoki mushrooms
    (optional)

To make the wontons: Place the shrimp, soy sauce, ginger, salt, and egg white in a blender or food processor. Chop until well combined. Transfer the mixture to a small bowl and mix in the garlic, scallion, and red pepper. Divide the filling among the wonton skins, placing about 1 teaspoon of filling about 1 inch from one corner of each skin. Dip your fingers into water and lightly dampen the outside edges of the wontons. Fold up 1 corner of a wonton to cover the filling, then fold it over again. Turn the wonton so that the triangle is toward you. Dampen the left corner of the wonton with a little water. Fold the right corner over and affix it to the left corner, then pull stuffed center toward you. Repeat to fold all of the remaining wonton. Refrigerate until needed.

To make the soup: Cut the green part off the scallions and cut into thin diagonal slices. Trim the root end off the white part of the scallions. Make 4 or 5 lengthwise cuts through each scallion without going all the way through the bulb end. Spread the pieces apart and place the scallions in ice water to open up.

In a large pot, combine the chicken stock, soy sauce, and ginger. Bring to a boil and drop in the Chinese sausage and wontons. Cook for 3

minutes, then drop in the shrimp, zucchini, squash, carrot, and shiitake mushrooms. Boil for approximately 2 more minutes, or until the wontons are tender.

Divide the soup among 4 bowls and garnish with cilantro sprigs, enoki mushrooms, sliced scallions, and vegetable flowers.

Note: To make the vegetable flowers, cut four to six ⅛-inch channels down the sides of the vegetable pieces with a paring knife, then slice into flowers.

# Manhattan Clam Chowder

Serves 6 to 8

**Some say that the tomato version of chowder was invented on Long Island, where farmers and fishermen live in harmony. Others claim it is a takeoff on the hearty Neapolitan specialty *zuppa di vongole*.**

1½ to 2 quarts quahogs or chowder clams

1 tablespoon cornstarch

1 cup bottled clam juice

4 ounces salt pork or bacon, finely chopped

1 large onion, chopped

1 celery stalk, chopped

½ green pepper, seeded and chopped

1 large carrot, chopped

1 can (16 ounces) plum tomatoes, chopped, with juices

¼ teaspoon dried thyme

½ teaspoon salt

¼ teaspoon freshly ground black pepper

1 potato, peeled and diced

Dash of Tabasco

Scrub the clams and soak for 30 minutes in a large bowl of cold water to which you have added the cornstarch. Rinse well.

Place the clams in a large saucepan with the bottled clam juice. Heat to boiling, cover, and reduce the heat. Simmer until the clams open, 4 to 5 minutes. Remove the clams from their shells, adding any liquor to the pot. Chop the clams and set aside. Strain the liquid through cheesecloth or paper towels. Add water if necessary to make 3 cups.

Sauté the salt pork in a heavy saucepan over medium heat until very crisp and rendered of all fat, about 8 minutes. Transfer with a slotted spoon to a bowl.

Discard all but 1 tablespoon drippings and add the onion. Cook, scraping the bottom and sides of the pan, until the onion is lightly browned, about 5 minutes. Add the celery, pepper, carrot, tomatoes, thyme, salt, and pepper. Sauté gently for 5 minutes. Add the clam juice. Heat to boiling, reduce the heat, and simmer, covered, for 30 minutes. Add the potato and continue to cook, covered, for 20 minutes. Stir in the clams and add the Tabasco and more salt and pepper to taste.

# New England Clam Chowder

Serves 6

One of the greatest American food debates centers on clam chowder, or rather whether to use tomato in the recipe. New Englanders, for the most part, are highly offended at the idea and have, in fact, proposed laws banning the fruit from the dish. A typical New England recipe follows.

1½ to 2 quarts quahogs or chowder clams

1 tablespoon cornstarch

1½ cups water (or 1 cup bottled clam juice and ½ cup water)

3 pounds potatoes (about 6 medium), peeled and diced

4 ounces salt pork or bacon, diced

1 large onion, finely chopped

2 cups milk, scalded

2 tablespoons unsalted butter, softened

2 tablespoons all-purpose flour

2 cups heavy cream

Pinch of dried thyme

Salt

Freshly ground black pepper

Chopped fresh parsley

Scrub the clams and soak for 30 minutes in a large bowl of cold water to which you have added the cornstarch. Rinse well.

Place the clams and the water (or clam juice and water) in a large saucepan. Heat to boiling, cover, and reduce the heat. Simmer until the clams open, 4 or 5 minutes. Remove the clams from their shells, adding any liquor to the pot. Chop the clams and set aside. Strain the liquid through cheesecloth or paper towels and reserve.

Cook the potatoes in boiling salted water for 3 minutes. Drain.

Sauté the salt pork in a large heavy saucepan over medium-low heat until golden and rendered of fat. Remove all but 1 tablespoon fat from the pan and add the onion. Cook for 5 minutes. Stir in the milk, scraping the sides and bottom of the pan. Add the potatoes and strained clam liquid. Heat to boiling, reduce the heat, and simmer for 5 minutes.

Combine the butter with the flour until smooth and stir into the chowder. Add the cream and thyme. Heat to boiling, reduce the heat, and simmer until thickened, 5 to 10 minutes longer. Stir in the clams and cook 2 minutes longer. Add salt and pepper to taste. Sprinkle with parsley.

# Seafood Gumbo

Serves 10

A bowl full of this seafood gumbo is like a postcard from the bayou country, with its sweet crabmeat, rich shrimp, and aromatic peppers, all thickened with fresh okra. Variations are legion, but cooks generally agree that the key to a successful gumbo is starting with a good roux.

1 pound fresh, cooked blue crabmeat or other crabmeat such as Dungeness, picked over to remove cartilage and shell fragments

¾ cup vegetable oil

1¼ pounds fresh okra, thinly sliced crosswise

1½ cups coarsely chopped onion

½ cup coarsely chopped green pepper

½ cup finely chopped celery

¼ cup all-purpose flour

6 ounces canned tomato paste

6 cups water

1 teaspoon red pepper flakes

½ teaspoon cayenne

1 teaspoon paprika

3 cloves garlic, crushed

½ teaspoon dried thyme

1 tablespoon salt, or to taste

2 bay leaves

1 pound medium shrimp, peeled and deveined

10 cups hot cooked long-grain white rice for serving

10 fresh thyme sprigs for garnish (optional)

Place the crabmeat in a bowl. Using a fork, gently fluff but do not cut the crabmeat to separate it into bite-sized pieces. Set aside.

Heat ¼ cup of oil in a dutch oven over high heat. Add the okra to the hot oil and sauté until tender, 8 to 10 minutes. Reduce the heat to low and add the onion, bell pepper, and celery. Cook, stirring occasionally, until the vegetables are soft, 8 to 10 minutes. Remove the dutch oven from the heat and set aside.

To make the roux, in a large, heavy skillet over high heat, combine the remaining oil and the flour. Cook, stirring constantly, until chestnut brown, 4 to 6 minutes. Immediately transfer the roux to the vegetables in the dutch oven.

Add the tomato paste and water to the vegetables and stir until well blended. Stir in the red pepper flakes, cayenne, paprika, garlic, dried thyme, salt, and bay leaves. Set the dutch oven over medium heat, bring to a simmer, and cook, stirring occasionally, for 10 minutes. Stir in the crabmeat and shrimp. Cook just until the crabmeat is heated through and the shrimp turn pink and the interiors are opaque throughout, 1 to 2 minutes. Remove and discard the bay leaves.

To serve, fill individual soup bowls with the hot cooked rice and ladle the gumbo over. Garnish with thyme sprigs, if desired.

# 4
# Poultry

# Green Chile Soup

Serves 6

**This spicy soup is a perfect remedy for a cold or whatever ails. Homemade chicken stock rather than canned will make it even better. Serve this with warm corn tortillas.**

3 slices smoked bacon

I whole chicken breast, boned, skinned, and cut into ½-inch cubes

6 ounces boneless pork, cut into ½-inch cubes

4 tablespoons unsalted butter

I cup finely chopped onion

⅓ cup unbleached all-purpose flour

2 *chiles de árbol*, toasted, stemmed, seeded, and crushed, or I tablespoon dried chili powder

I teaspoon ground cumin

I garlic clove, minced

6 cups warm Chicken Stock (page 126)

6 Anaheim or New Mexico green chiles, roasted, peeled, cored, seeded, and diced

I jalapeño pepper, seeded and minced

I red pepper, roasted, peeled, cored, seeded, and diced

2 large ripe tomatoes, diced

I tablespoon minced fresh cilantro

Salt

Freshly ground black pepper

Grated Cheddar or Monterey Jack cheese for garnish (optional)

Tortillas

Heat a large, heavy skillet over medium-high heat; add the bacon and cook until crisp. Remove the bacon with a slotted spoon, drain on paper towels, crumble, and reserve. Add the chicken and pork cubes to the hot bacon fat and sauté until brown, about 5 minutes. Drain and set aside.

In a large, heavy pot, melt the butter; add the onion and sauté until softened. Stir in the flour and cook for 2 to 3 minutes, stirring constantly; add the crushed *chiles de árbol*, cumin, and garlic and continue cooking, stirring, for another minute. Slowly add the warm chicken stock, whisking until the mixture is smooth and thickened. Add the green chiles, peppers, tomatoes, cilantro, bacon, pork, and chicken to the soup; add salt and pepper. Lower the heat and simmer for 10 minutes, or until flavors are blended and the soup is hot. Divide among 6 bowls, garnish with grated cheese, if desired, and serve with warm tortillas.

*Mexico*

# Chicken Soup
*Caldo de Pollo*
Serves 6 to 8

**Eaten everywhere in Mexico, this simple, nourishing soup is often served as a main course. The vegetables may vary, but the soup is almost always served with lime, chopped onions, and green chiles.**

**For the Stock:**

1 whole chicken, about 3 pounds, cut into serving pieces

1 whole carrot

4 cloves garlic

1 tablespoon salt

6 black peppercorns

1 small sprig parsley

1 small onion, quartered

**For the Soup:**

1/4 cup canned or cooked chick-peas

1 chayote, peeled and quartered

1 large potato, peeled and cut into chunks

2 ears corn, each cut into 3 pieces

2 carrots, thickly sliced

1 cup sliced cabbage

2 sprigs cilantro

1 sprig spearmint

1 cup cooked rice (optional)

3 limes, sliced

4 chiles serranos, seeds and membranes removed, and chopped

½ cup chopped onion

To make the stock: Rinse the chicken and giblets and place in a large pot or dutch oven. Add 10 cups of water, whole carrot, garlic, salt, peppercorns, parsley, and onion. Bring to a boil, skim the surface, cover, and cook over medium heat for 1 hour. Let cool, remove the chicken, and degrease the stock.

To make the soup: Add the chick-peas after the stock has cooked for only 30 minutes. Cook 30 more minutes, then discard the parsley, onion, and whole carrot. Add the chayote, potato, corn, sliced carrots, cabbage, cilantro, and spearmint. Cover and cook over medium heat for 30 minutes, or until the vegetables are tender.

To serve, put a piece of chicken and some vegetables in each bowl, add some rice if you like, and pour the hot broth over. Pass the lime slices and chopped chiles and onion separately.

# Chicken Ball and Pea Soup

Serves 6

5 ounces chicken breast meat

1 egg white, lightly beaten

1 tablespoon cornstarch

½ cup ice water

½ teaspoon salt

2 cups oil for deep-frying

4 cups Chicken Stock
(page 126)

2 teaspoons rice wine or dry
sherry

1 cup fresh peas, cooked

1 tablespoon rendered chicken
fat, melted (optional)

Reduce the chicken meat to a paste with a cleaver or in a food processor. Add the egg white, cornstarch, and ice water and season with the salt. Stir in one direction only. The mixture should be so smooth and moist that the chicken paste falls from a chopstick in large droplets.

Heat the oil in a wok and reduce the heat. Pour the chicken paste into a funnel and allow it to drip into the hot fat in drops about the size of green peas. Fry until just white and cooked through, then lift out with a slotted spoon and drain.

Heat the chicken stock and add the rice wine. Then add the drained peas and the chicken balls and heat through. Season with salt to taste. Add the chicken fat, if used, and serve.

# Chicken Soup
# with Matzo Balls

Serves 8 to 10

**Chicken soup appears in many cuisines enriched with rice, noodles, dumplings, wontons, and the like. Matzo balls are used in Jewish communities around the world.**

**For the Soup:**

1 chicken, 3½ to 4 pounds

6 cups Chicken Stock (page 126)

1 whole onion, unpeeled

1 garlic clove

1 carrot, roughly chopped

1 celery stalk with leaves, broken

1 white turnip, chopped

1 parsnip, chopped

4 whole cloves

1 bay leaf

3 parsley sprigs

½ teaspoon freshly ground pepper

1 teaspoon red wine vinegar

Chopped fresh dill

Matzo balls

**For the Matzo Balls:**

3 eggs

6 tablespoons cold club soda

3 tablespoons cold chicken fat

½ teaspoon salt

pinch of ground white pepper

¾ cup matzo meal (approximately)

With sharp scissors, remove the fat and excess skin from the cavity and neck area of the chicken. Cut off the wing tips. Peel the neck and scrape off the fat. You should have about ⅔ cup fat. Refrigerate the chicken, covered.

Place the chicken fat, skin, and wing tips in a small saucepan and add ⅓ cup water. Simmer slowly over low heat for about 30 minutes. As the water is absorbed, it will be replaced by chicken fat in the pan. When the fat begins to sizzle, it is rendered. Remove 3 tablespoons for use in the matzo ball recipe. Chill for 30 minutes.

To make the soup: Place the chicken in a large heavy pot or dutch oven. Add the stock, onion, garlic, carrot, celery, turnip, parsnip, cloves, bay leaf, parsley, and pepper. Add water to cover, heat to boiling, and reduce the heat. Simmer the soup over medium-low heat, skimming the surface as needed, until the chicken is very tender, about 1 hour.

Remove the chicken and carefully separate the meat from bones. Save the meat for another use. Return the bones to the soup and add the vinegar. Simmer 15 minutes longer. Let cool and strain into a clean pot, discarding all the solids.

To serve, heat the soup to boiling. Reduce the heat, and simmer for 10 minutes. Sprinkle with dill. Add matzo balls. Ladle soup into bowls.

To make the matzo balls: Lightly beat the eggs in a bowl. Beat in the club soda, fat and salt and pepper. Slowly beat in ¼ cup of the matzo meal. Add more matzo meal, 2 tablespoons at a time, until the mixture has the texture of soft mashed potatoes. Refrigerate, covered, for at least 2 hours.

Heat 3 quarts of water to boiling. With wet hands, shape the matzo mixture into balls about 1½ inches in diameter. Drop into the water and reduce the heat to medium. Simmer for 25–35 minutes. Remove the matzo balls with a slotted spoon and place 1 in each soup bowl. You can also let cool and reheat in the soup.

# Ray's Old-Fashioned Chicken 'n' Dumplings

Serves 8

To Ray L. Overton III, an Atlanta teacher and food writer, this recipe represents the Old South. "It has been in my family for generations, beginning with my great-grandma Maude who learned to make it from her mother shortly before her wedding day," Overton says. "Especially popular during the Great Depression, it was a dish that could be stretched to serve a crowd after church simply by adding a little more flour, lard or chicken fat, and water to the dumpling recipe. Over the years, it has been refined and adapted to suit the tastes of different family members."

**For the Chicken Stock:**

1 frying chicken, about 4 pounds, cut into 8 pieces

1 onion, quartered

1 large carrot, cut into 4 pieces

1 celery stalk, cut into 4 pieces

1 bay leaf

1 teaspoon salt

1 teaspoon whole black peppercorns

1 sprig each of fresh parsley, sage, rosemary, and thyme, tied together with kitchen twine

**For the Dumplings:**

3 cups sifted all-purpose flour

$\frac{1}{2}$ teaspoon baking soda

$\frac{1}{2}$ teaspoon salt

6 tablespoons vegetable shortening or lard, chilled

$\frac{1}{4}$ cup chicken stock (from this recipe)

$\frac{2}{3}$ cup low-fat buttermilk

1 tablespoon minced fresh thyme or 2 teaspoons dried thyme

Salt

Freshly ground black pepper

To make the stock: Place the chicken pieces in a large, heavy stockpot with enough water to cover by 1 inch (2–3 quarts). Add the onion, carrot, celery, bay leaf, salt, peppercorns, and fresh herb bouquet. Bring to a boil over high heat. Reduce the heat to low and simmer for $1\frac{1}{2}$ to 2 hours, stirring occasionally and skimming and discarding any foam that rises to the top.

Remove the chicken from the pot and set aside to cool. When cool enough to handle, skin and bone the chicken; cut the meat into bite-sized pieces and set aside. Return the skin and bones to the pot and simmer for 1 hour longer. Strain the stock, discarding the solids, and return the stock to the pot. If desired, reserve the vegetables (discarding the bay leaf, peppercorns, and fresh herb bouquet) to add back to the pot just before serving. Refrigerate the stock for at least 1 hour or overnight. Skim and discard any fat that has risen to the top.

To make the dumplings: Sift together in a large bowl the flour, baking soda, and salt. Add the shortening or lard and, using a pastry blender, 2 knives, or a fork, cut into the flour mixture until it resembles coarse meal. Make a well in the center of the mixture and add the $\frac{1}{4}$ cup chicken stock, the buttermilk, and thyme.

Stir until well blended and a stiff dough forms. On a lightly floured work surface, knead the dough gently 8 to 10 times. Pat the dough into a flat disk, wrap tightly in plastic wrap, and refrigerate for at least 1 hour or overnight.

Bring the stock to a slow simmer over medium-low heat. On a lightly floured work surface, roll out the chilled dough about ⅛ inch thick. Sprinkle the work surface with more flour if the dough begins to stick. Cut the dough into 1-inch-square dumplings. Drop the dumplings, one at a time, into the simmering stock. When all the dumplings have been added to the stock, stir gently and cook until the dumplings are tender but with a slight bite, 10 to 12 minutes. Add the reserved chicken meat, reserved vegetables, if desired, salt, and pepper and stir gently. Serve at once.

# 5
## Meat

# Lamb and Bean Soup
*Harira*

Serves 6

**Muslims serve this hearty soup to break the fast at the end of Ramadan. There are many variations on this recipe. All of them are lemony, some omit the eggs, some have only lentils, and still others add noodles or orzo.**

½ cup dried chick-peas

Salt

⅔ cup lentils

3 tablespoons white rice

3 tablespoons all-purpose flour mixed with ½ cup water

2 tablespoons unsalted butter

1 tablespoon olive oil

½ pound lamb, cut into ½-inch cubes

2 onions, chopped

2 garlic cloves, finely minced

½ teaspoon ground ginger

1 teaspoon ground cinnamon

½ teaspoon ground turmeric

2 cups puréed canned plum tomatoes or 1½ pounds peeled, seeded, and chopped fresh plum tomatoes

½ cup chopped fresh flat-leaf parsley

¼ cup chopped fresh cilantro

2 teaspoons freshly ground black pepper

2 eggs

¼ cup fresh lemon juice

Place the chick-peas in a bowl with water to cover generously. Refrigerate overnight. Drain and rinse well.

Transfer the chick-peas to a 1-quart saucepan and add 3 cups of water. Bring to a boil, reduce the heat to low, cover, and simmer until cooked through but not falling apart, about 1 hour. Remove from the heat and salt lightly. Drain the chick-peas, reserving the cooking liquid. You will have about 1½ cups chick-peas. Set the chick-peas and liquid aside.

Pour another 3 cups of water into a 3-quart saucepan and bring to a boil. Add the lentils and rice and simmer for 20 minutes. Add the flour-water paste, stirring in well.

While the lentils are simmering, in a large sauté pan over high heat, melt the butter with the oil. Add the lamb and brown well on all sides, about 5 minutes. Add the onions, garlic, ginger, cinnamon and turmeric and sauté for a few minutes. Add the remaining 3 cups water and simmer, uncovered, over low heat for 30 minutes.

Add the meat-onion mixture, drained chick-peas, tomatoes, parsley, and cilantro to the lentils and simmer for 15 minutes. Add salt to taste and the pepper; the soup should be

peppery. If it seems too thick, thin it with a little of the reserved cooking liquid. Remove the soup from the heat.

In a small bowl whisk together the eggs and lemon juice. Stir into the soup. Serve at once.

# Aromatic Braised Beef with Noodles in Rich Broth

*Bo Bun Hue*

Serves 6 to 8

The backbone of the Vietnamese cuisine consists of soup/noodle combinations. Served in deep bowls, they are a meal in themselves and are enjoyed throughout the day. Chicken, pork, shrimp, and fish are all served in this way, but perhaps the most common ingredient in these hearty dishes is beef. It comes in varying guises—braised in rich anise-scented broth, thinly sliced and fried with onions, or simply simmered in water with ginger and chiles or fish sauce. It rests atop a generous tangle of tender noodles—rice vermicelli, egg noodles, or ribbons of rice noodles. Aromatics and vegetables add to an already hearty meal.

1½ pounds braising beef

1½ pounds beef shank

6 slices fresh ginger

2 pieces dried tangerine peel (optional)

4 whole star anise

1 medium onion

Salt

1½ pounds thick fresh egg noodles

8 scallions

4 ounces fresh bean sprouts

Chopped fresh cilantro

*Nuoc cham* (dipping sauce; recipe follows)

*Nuoc mam* (fish sauce)

Cut the beef and shank into large pieces. Place in a large saucepan and add the ginger, tangerine peel if used, star anise, halved onion, and 12 cups of water. Bring to the boil. Skim off the froth, reduce the heat, and simmer, partially covered, for about 2½ hours, until the stock is well flavored. Add salt to taste and keep hot.

Drop the noodles into a large pot of well-salted water and boil for about 2 minutes until tender. Drain and divide among 6 to 8 deep bowls.

Trim and chop the scallions. Blanch the bean sprouts for 30 seconds; drain. Add a little of each to the bowls. Strain in the hot stock, then add several pieces of beef (the beef should be tender enough to break up with two forks).

Add a sprinkling of chopped cilantro and serve with dishes of *nuoc cham* and *nuoc mam*.

# Nuoc Cham

Serves 6

1 fresh red chile, seeded and
   shredded

1 ½ tablespoons lime juice

¼ cup *nuoc mam*

¼ cup water

2 teaspoons sugar, or to taste

1 tablespoon crushed roasted
   peanuts

1 tablespoon finely slivered
   carrot

Mix the sauce ingredients together and divide
among several small dishes.

# Fried Egg Soup with Pork
*Gaeng Jued Kai*

Serves 4

**Easy to prepare, this mild-flavored soup is a good accompaniment for any meal.**

¼ cup oil

4 garlic cloves, chopped

½ cup chopped onions

6 eggs, beaten

8 ounces pork, thinly sliced in 2-inch lengths

⅓ cup *nam pla* (fish sauce)

I cup sliced cabbage

2 scallions, cut into 1-inch lengths

¼ teaspoon white pepper

Heat a small skillet and add half the oil. Fry the garlic until golden brown. Set aside the garlic, then fry the onion.

To another small skillet add the rest of the oil and fry the beaten eggs until golden brown, about 2 minutes on each side. Remove carefully, keeping it in one piece, and set aside. When cool, cut into 1-inch by 2-inch strips.

In a large saucepan, heat 6 cups of water to boiling and add the pork. Reheat to boiling and when the pork is cooked add the egg strips, onion, and the remaining ingredients. Remove to a serving bowl and top with the fried garlic before serving.

# Hot Chili Beef and Onion Soup

*Yukkai Jang Kuk*

Serves 6 to 8

**This chili-red soup is exceptionally hot. It is said that the time to serve it is in the hottest months, when the perspiration it induces has a cooling effect on the diner. It is equally effective ammunition against winter cold.**

1 pound braising beef

1½ tablespoons hot chili powder

2 tablespoons sesame oil

12 scallions

2 teaspoons crushed garlic

1 tablespoon white sesame seeds, toasted and ground

1 teaspoon sugar

½ teaspoon white pepper

1½ tablespoons dark soy sauce

Cut the beef into cubes and place in a saucepan with 8 cups of water. Bring to a boil, reduce the heat, and simmer gently for 1½ to 2 hours, until the meat is falling apart.

Mix the chili powder with the sesame oil. Trim and shred the scallions. Heat the chili powder and sesame oil in a pan and fry the scallions with the garlic for 2 minutes. Add the sesame seeds, sugar, pepper and soy sauce and fry for 2 to 3 minutes over medium heat.

Lift out the meat, drain well, and toss in the pan with the seasonings for a few minutes. Return the contents of the pan to the stock and bring to the boil, simmering until the soup is well flavored.

# Noodles with Assorted Sliced Meats and Fish in Soup
*Banh Cahn Tom Cua*

Serves 6 to 8

4 ounces fresh bacon or
    pancetta with rind

4 ounces chicken breast
    meat

4 ounces peeled shrimp

4 ounces cooked crabmeat

4 ounces cleaned squid

4 ounces thin egg noodles

6 cups Chicken Stock
    (page 126)

4 scallions

Salt

White pepper

2 shallots

2 tablespoons vegetable oil

2 tablespoons chopped fresh
    cilantro

*Nuoc cham* (page 93) or
    *Nuoc mam* (fish sauce)

Bring a saucepan of lightly salted water to the boil. Put in the fresh bacon or pancetta and simmer for about 30 minutes, until tender, then add the chicken and cook a further 15 minutes. Lift the meat out and discard the stock. Set the meat aside until cool enough to handle.

Devein the shrimp, using a wooden pick to ease the vein gently through an incision in the center back. Separate the crabmeat into small chunks. Cut the squid into thin rings, if small, or into small squares if larger, scoring these diagonally at close intervals on one side to tenderize.

Drop the noodles into a pot of simmering salted water and cook briefly, then drain well.

Cut the bacon and chicken into thin slices. Bring the stock to the boil and add the meat and seafood. Chop the scallions and add half to the pot with salt and white pepper to taste. Simmer gently for 6 minutes.

Finely chop the shallots and fry in the oil until almost crisp. Pour the soup into a tureen, add the noodles, and garnish with the remaining scallions, the cilantro, and fried shallots. Serve with *nuoc cham* or *nuoc mam*.

# Posole

Serves 6

Posole, a traditional dish in New Mexico, is a rustic stew made of hominy, pork, dried New Mexico red chile pods, and spices. Served by the Pueblo people on feast days and New Year's Day, it is often accompanied with Red Chile Sauce and bread or tortillas. In Latino markets, hominy (limed whole corn) is available dried or canned.

1½ cups dried hominy, soaked overnight in water and drained, or two 16-ounce cans hominy, rinsed and drained (about 3 cups)

1½ pounds lean boneless pork, cut into ½-inch cubes

2 dried New Mexico red chiles, stems and seeds removed, torn into pieces

2 cups finely chopped onions

3 garlic cloves, minced

2 teaspoons minced fresh oregano, or 1 teaspoon dried oregano

1 teaspoon cumin seed, crushed

Salt

Red Chile Sauce (recipe follows) or cored, seeded, and minced jalapeño peppers for garnish

In a large pot, combine with 6 cups of water all the ingredients except the salt and the red chile sauce or jalapeños. Bring to a boil over medium-high heat; lower heat and simmer, uncovered, for 2 to 3 hours, or until the meat is tender and the hominy kernels have burst and are swelled and tender. The stew should have plenty of liquid, so add more water if necessary throughout the cooking time.

Divide the hominy among 6 bowls and pass the chile sauce or jalapeños.

# Red Chile Sauce

Makes about 2 cups

This classic sauce is used in enchiladas, huevos rancheros, tamales, soups, beans, and so on; it is also an excellent marinade for steak or chicken. New Mexico green chiles turn red when they dry, and are strung together decoratively in cascades called *ristras*.

*Posole*

10 whole dried New Mexico
    chiles
1 tablespoon olive oil
1 cup finely chopped onions
2 garlic cloves, minced
2 cups Chicken Stock
    (page 126)
2 tablespoons vegetable oil
Salt

Preheat the oven to 250°F.

Place the chiles in a heavy skillet and roast them dry in the hot oven for 3 to 4 minutes, being careful not to let them burn.

Fill a pot just large enough to hold the chiles with water; bring the water to a boil and remove from the heat. Add the roasted chiles to the hot water and, using a weight such as a pot lid, keep them submerged until they are soft, about 20 or 30 minutes. Remove the chiles from the water and stem, seed, and tear them into strips.

Heat the olive oil in a medium skillet over low heat; add the onion and sauté until browned, about 5 minutes.

Put the chile strips, sautéed onion, garlic, and 1 cup of the chicken stock into a food processor or a blender and purée until smooth; strain.

Heat the vegetable oil in a heavy skillet over medium heat. Add the chile mixture to the hot oil and cook, stirring, for about 5 minutes. Add chicken stock until the sauce is the desired consistency. Add salt to taste. Cover and refrigerate until ready to use. Keeps 2 to 3 days, refrigerated.

# Scotch Broth

Serves 4 to 6

**This hearty homemade soup makes a memorable meal served with crusty bread and a salad. Scotch Broth lends itself to ahead-of-time cooking and will keep in the refrigerator for 3 to 4 days. Thin with chicken stock if necessary.**

**For the Stock:**

1½ to 2 pounds lamb shoulder steaks or other lean lamb with bones

Flour seasoned with salt and pepper

3 tablespoons olive oil or vegetable oil

½ cup chopped carrot

½ cups chopped onion

½ cup chopped celery

2 large garlic cloves, minced

1 teaspoon sugar

¼ cup chopped fresh parsley

1 bay leaf

One 3-inch sprig fresh thyme, or ½ teaspoon dried thyme

¾ teaspoon salt

8 to 10 whole peppercorns

**For the Soup:**

Strained stock

½ cup pearl barley

2 large carrots, diced

1 small white turnip, julienned

Salt

Freshly ground black pepper

Parsley and grated lemon zest, for garnish

To make the stock: Trim the meat of any fat and dredge it lightly in the seasoned flour. Heat the oil in a heavy skillet, add the meat and bones, and brown well. Transfer to a soup kettle.

In the same skillet, sauté the chopped carrot, onion, celery, and garlic in the meat drippings for 1 to 2 minutes. Sprinkle the sugar over the vegetables and continue to cook, stirring constantly. The vegetables should caramelize slightly but not burn. Add the vegetables to the meat and bones.

Stir about 1 cup of water into the skillet, scrape up the drippings, and pour them over the meat and vegetables. Add 5 cups of water, parsley, bay leaf, thyme, salt, and peppercorns. Cover and bring to a boil. Reduce the heat and simmer slowly for 2 hours, or until the meat is tender. Strain the stock and degrease. Remove the meat from the bones, dice, and reserve.

To make the soup: Combine the strained stock and pearl barley in the soup kettle and cook for 30 minutes. Add the reserved meat and diced carrots and the turnip and cook an additional 20 minutes, or until the vegetables are tender. Add salt and pepper to taste.

Serve garnished with fresh parsley and a pinch of lemon zest.

# Beef and Barley Soup
Serves 6 to 8

**This soup recipe is a descendant of the ones brought to this country by Russian immigrants, although the good folks in Montana, where barley grows in abundance, stir up a very similar potful.**

2 tablespoons vegetable oil

1¼ pounds stewing beef, cut into 1-inch cubes

1 garlic clove

5 cups water

½ cup boiling water

½ ounce dried mushrooms

1 small onion, chopped

1 carrot, chopped

1½ large celery stalks, chopped

1 large tomato, peeled, seeded, and chopped (about 1 cup)

½ teaspoon sugar

1 small parsnip, chopped

1 small white turnip, chopped

Pinch of dried thyme

¼ cup dried pearl barley

4 cups Beef Stock (page 127)

Salt

Freshly ground black pepper

Chopped fresh parsley (optional)

Heat the oil in a large heavy pot or dutch oven over medium-high heat. Sauté the meat until well browned on all sides. Add the garlic and 1 quart water, stirring and scraping the bottom and sides of the pot. Heat to boiling, reduce the heat, and simmer, partially covered, for 1 hour. Skim the surface of grease as it rises to the top.

Meanwhile, pour the boiling water over the mushrooms in a small bowl. Let stand for 20 minutes.

Add the mushrooms with their liquid to the soup. Add the onion, carrot, celery, tomato, sugar, parsnip, turnip, thyme, barley, stock, and remaining 1 cup water. Simmer, partially covered, until the meat is very tender, about 1¼ hours. If the soup becomes too thick, add water. Add salt and pepper to taste. Sprinkle with parsley if you like.

# Kentucky Burgoo

Serves 12 to 14

In Owensboro, Kentucky, barbecued mutton has long been the major food attraction of political rallies and other outdoor gatherings. Often the leftovers go into a bubbling black pot of burgoo, the Kentucky version of Brunswick Stew, which is typically served as a side dish to the barbecue. At home, it makes a hearty main dish that produces heavenly kitchen scents for hours as it simmers.

1 pound lean beef chuck or round, cut into 1-inch cubes

½ pound lean lamb, cut into 1-inch cubes

1 pound skinless, boneless chicken breasts, cut crosswise into ½-inch strips

2 quarts Beef Stock (page 127) or Vegetable Stock (page 128)

1 cup diced boiling potatoes

1 cup finely chopped onion

1 cup fresh or frozen lima beans

2 green peppers, finely chopped

4 carrots, thinly sliced

1 cup fresh or frozen corn kernels

1 tablespoon salt, or to taste

1 teaspoon cayenne

½ teaspoon freshly ground black pepper

1 cup thinly sliced fresh okra

6 tomatoes, peeled, seeded, and coarsely chopped

2 garlic cloves, crushed

2 tablespoons apple cider vinegar

Sprigs of fresh parsley for garnish (optional)

In a large, heavy, nonreactive pot over high heat, combine the beef, lamb, chicken, and stock and bring to a boil. Reduce the heat to low, cover, and simmer, stirring occasionally, for 1½ hours.

Add the potatoes, onion, lima beans, bell peppers, carrots, and corn and stir until well blended. Stir in the salt, cayenne, and pepper to taste. Cover and continue to simmer, stirring occasionally, for 3 hours longer.

Add the okra, tomatoes, garlic, and vinegar and stir until well blended. Cover and simmer, stirring occasionally, until the meat, poultry, and vegetables are fork-tender and the flavors have melded, about 2 hours longer. Add a little water while cooking if the stew is sticking or is thicker than desired.

To serve, ladle the burgoo into individual soup bowls and garnish with parsley, if desired. Serve hot.

# 6
# Cold
# Soups

# Yogurt Soup

*Caçik*
Serves 4

**A refreshing summer soup popular in Greece and the Balkans, as well as Turkey. Without the water, this makes a delightful summer salad.**

2 cups plain yogurt

I garlic clove, finely minced

I large cucumber, peeled, seeded, and shredded or finely diced

3 tablespoons chopped toasted walnuts

½ cup chopped fresh mint

Salt

Freshly ground black pepper

Ice water

Fresh chives, mint, or sage

In a bowl combine all of the ingredients except the ice water. Cover and refrigerate for 2 to 4 hours.

At serving time, thin with ice water to desired consistency. Taste and adjust the seasoning, then ladle into individual bowls and serve immediately, garnished with a fresh herb.

# Gazpacho

Serves 12

**Of Spanish heritage, this dish is really a salad in soup form. (According to James Beard, a recipe for "gaspacho" appeared under Salads in Mary Randolph's book, *The Virginia Housewife,* in 1836.) It depends on good ripe tomatoes, in season, and a cook patient about wielding a knife—the food processor tends to do a coarse, uneven job of chopping. It is ideal for a picnic or barbecue.**

3 pounds ripe tomatoes

2 garlic cloves, minced

2 English cucumbers, halved, seeded, and diced

½ medium green pepper, minced

½ medium red pepper, minced

1 medium red onion, minced

2 celery stalks, minced

¼ cup olive oil

¼ cup red wine vinegar

2 cups, more or less, well-seasoned tomato juice

Salt

Freshly ground black pepper

Tabasco

Peel the tomatoes and cut them in half horizontally. Working over a colander set in a large bowl, scoop out most of the seeds and juice from the insides. Discard the seeds, which will remain in the colander, but save the juice in the bowl. Finely chop the tomatoes and place them in the bowl with their juice.

Add the garlic and combine well, then stir in the cucumbers, peppers, onion, and celery.

In another bowl, whisk the olive oil and vinegar together, then add 2 cups of tomato juice. Add this mixture to the vegetables and stir to blend. If necessary, add more tomato juice to obtain the consistency of soup, not salad. Season with salt, pepper, and Tabasco to taste. Chill thoroughly before serving.

# Melon Soup
*Sopa de Melon*

Serves 4

**Starting a meal with a cool fruit soup is an untraditional but highly satisfactory prelude to a spicy main dish.**

3 ripe cantaloupes

2 tablespoons honey

¼ cup fresh lemon juice

½ cup fresh orange juice

¼ cup port

Cut the cantaloupes in half, remove and discard the seeds, then scoop out the pulp, being careful not to tear the peel. Set the 6 cantaloupe shells aside.

Roughly chop the cantaloupe pulp and purée in a blender with the honey, lemon juice, orange juice, and port.

Chill well before serving. Use the cantaloupe shells as soup bowls.

# Cucumber Soup
*Naing Kuk*
Serves 4 to 6

2 medium cucumbers, each
about 6 inches long

2 tablespoons light soy sauce

1½ tablespoons white vinegar

1 tablespoon chopped scallions

½ teaspoon sugar

½ teaspoon chili powder

1½ teaspoons sesame oil

5 cups Chicken Stock
(page 126)

2 teaspoons white sesame seeds

Peel the cucumbers and slice very thin. Place in a bowl and add the soy sauce, vinegar, scallions, sugar, chili powder, and sesame oil. Set aside for 1 hour, then add the chicken stock.

Toast the sesame seeds in a small pan over medium heat until they turn golden and begin to pop; then grind fine.

Transfer the soup to a tureen and sprinkle on the sesame seeds. Serve at room temperature or slightly chilled.

# Strawberry and Peach Soup

Serves 8

By varying the fruits in this recipe, you can make soup from any ripe, sweet fruit. This one is slightly sweet and creamy, with a good berry flavor, and is refreshing on a hot day.

4 cups hulled sliced
   strawberries

¼ cup sugar

Pinch of salt

2 tablespoons lemon juice

½ cup plain yogurt

½ cup heavy cream

1½ cups cold weak tea or water

½ cup dry white wine

2 large peaches, peeled, pitted,
   and finely diced

Place the strawberries in a food processor and purée until smooth, or purée them through the finest disk of a food mill.

Transfer to a bowl, add the sugar, salt, and lemon juice, then whisk in the yogurt, cream, tea, and wine. Taste, and add more sugar if necessary, but do not make it too sweet—it should taste fresh. Stir in the peaches and chill thoroughly before serving.

# Orange-Tomato Soup with Melons, Blueberries, and Grapes

Serves 6

This soup is a fruit version of the traditional gazpacho made with vegetables. Served with a hearty bread and a salad, it makes a perfect summer meal, or it may be served anytime as a first course.

1 ½ cups canned tomato purée

2 cups fresh orange juice

1 teaspoon sugar

2 teaspoons grated orange zest

1 teaspoon grated lime zest

1 ½ cups diced cantaloupe

1 ½ cups diced honeydew melon

¾ cup diced apple

¾ cup blueberries

¾ cup halved seedless green grapes

1 cup fresh strawberries, hulled and halved

1 kiwi, peeled and sliced

Put the tomato purée, orange juice, sugar, zests, half of the cantaloupe, and half of the honeydew melon in a food processor or blender. Process until smooth.

Pour the tomato mixture into a large nonaluminum bowl. Add the remaining cantaloupe and honeydew, apple, blueberries, and green grapes. Cover and refrigerate for at least 2 hours or overnight.

Divide the soup among 6 bowls. Garnish with the strawberries and kiwi.

# Apple Soup

Serves 6

4 tart apples, such as Granny
Smith, peeled, cored, and
quartered

I cup dry white wine

2 cinnamon sticks

3 slices fresh ginger

5 tablespoons sugar

I tablespoon Calvados or
applejack

¼ cup sour cream

I cup Beef Stock (page 127)

I cup heavy cream

2 tablespoons fresh lemon juice

¼ teaspoon salt

½ cup finely julienned apple
tossed with 2 tablespoons
fresh lemon juice, for garnish

Place the quartered apples, wine, cinnamon sticks, ginger, and sugar in a heavy saucepan. Over medium-high heat, bring to a boil. Cover, lower heat to medium, and simmer for 10 minutes. Let cool; discard the cinnamon sticks and ginger.

Place the cooked apples and the liquid in which they were cooked in a food processor or blender. Add the Calvados or applejack and sour cream; process until smooth. With the machine running, add the beef stock, then the cream, in a slow steady stream. Add the lemon juice and salt. Cover and refrigerate until chilled thoroughly.

Divide the soup among 6 chilled bowls and garnish with julienned apple.

# Cream of Tomato Soup

Serves 6

Creamy tomato soups are particularly suited for the summer months, when tomatoes are at their peak. New Jersey soil produces some of the best tomatoes grown in the country.

2 tablespoons vegetable oil

1 onion, chopped

1 garlic clove, minced

¼ teaspoon ground mace

2 tablespoons all-purpose flour

3 cups hot Chicken Stock
   (page 126)

2 pounds ripe tomatoes,
   coarsely chopped

½ teaspoon sugar

½ cup sour cream

Salt

Freshly ground white pepper

Chopped fresh chives

Heat the oil in a heavy saucepan over medium-low heat. Add the onion, garlic, and mace. Cook, covered, for 5 minutes. Do not let brown.

Sprinkle the onion mixture with the flour and cook, stirring constantly, for 2 minutes. Whisk in the hot stock and add the tomatoes and sugar. Heat to boiling, reduce the heat, and simmer, uncovered, for 20 minutes. Let cool to room temperature.

Transfer the soup in batches to a blender or food processor. Blend until smooth, then pour through a sieve into a bowl. Whisk in the sour cream and add salt and pepper to taste. Chill thoroughly and sprinkle with chopped chives before serving.

# Vichyssoise

Serves 6 to 8

America's most popular summer soup was invented around 1917 at the Ritz-Carlton Hotel by French chef Louis Diat. Basically, he turned his mother's leek and potato soup into creamy bliss and named it after Vichy, the town near where he grew up. This recipe is based on the original from Diat's *Cooking à la Ritz* (1941).

4 tablespoons unsalted butter

3 leeks, trimmed of green, washed well and sliced

1 onion, chopped

2½ pounds potatoes (about 5 medium), peeled and sliced

4 cups Chicken Stock (page 126)

2 cups milk

2 cups light cream or half-and-half

1 cup heavy cream

Salt

Freshly ground white pepper

Chopped fresh chives

Melt the butter in a large heavy saucepan over medium-low heat. Add the leeks and onion and cook until lightly browned, about 8 minutes. Stir in the potatoes and stock. Heat to boiling and boil for 30 minutes. Let cool slightly.

Place the leek-potato mixture in batches in a food processor or blender. Process until smooth and return to the saucepan. Add the milk and light cream and heat to boiling. Remove from the heat and let cool to room temperature.

Pour the soup through a sieve into a serving bowl. Stir in the heavy cream and salt and pepper to taste. Chill thoroughly and sprinkle with chives before serving.

*Vichyssoise, top.*
*Avocado Soup (page 122), bottom.*

# Avocado Soup

Serves 4 to 6

**The Aztecs were eating avocados long before Spanish settlers brought the fruit to the American Southwest. Avocados easily took hold in California and were introduced into Florida in 1833. The following soup is best made with the dark-skinned California variety. Do not serve it ice-cold or the delicate balance of flavors will be muted.**

3 cups Chicken Stock
(page 126)

3 ripe avocados (dark-skinned California or Hass variety), peeled and pitted

1 tablespoon lemon juice

2 cups heavy cream

Dash Tabasco

Salt

Freshly ground white pepper

1 teaspoon chopped fresh chervil or parsley

Place 2 cups of the stock in a food processor or blender. Cut the avocados directly into the stock, add the lemon juice, and process until smooth. Transfer to a bowl and add the remaining 1 cup stock and the cream. Chill.

Before serving, add Tabasco, salt, and white pepper to taste. Sprinkle with chervil.

*(photograph on page 121)*

# Chile Poblano and Almond Soup

*Sopa de Chile Poblano y Almendras*

Serves 6

**An unusual Mexican variation of the Spanish *gazpacho blanco,* mingling the almonds from Spain with the native chile poblano, this cold soup is from Mexico City chef María Dolores Torres Yzábal.**

8 chiles poblanos, about 2
  pounds

¼ cup olive oil

3 cloves garlic, crushed

6 ounces blanched almonds

5 cups Chicken Stock
  (page 126)

Pinch ground cumin

Salt

6 cooked shrimp, whole or
  diced, for garnish (optional)

Roast the chiles, peel, and remove the seeds and membranes. In a food processor or by hand, chop the chiles fine, being careful not to purée. Heat the oil in a large saucepan or dutch oven, add the garlic and, before it browns, add the chiles. Cook over medium heat for about 5 minutes, stirring constantly so that the chiles do not stick to the bottom of the pan.

Grind the almonds with some chicken stock in a blender or processor until very fine. Add this and the remaining stock to the chiles, add cumin and salt to taste, and let simmer over low heat for 10 minutes. Remove from the heat.

Refrigerate until completely cold and add the shrimp, if desired. This soup tastes better when prepared a day before serving.

# 7
# Basic Stocks

# Chicken Stock

Makes about 3 quarts

1 large chicken or fowl

2 onions, peeled and halved

2 carrots, scraped and
    quartered

2 celery stalks, quartered, plus
    a few celery leaves

6 parsley sprigs tied together
    with 1 bay leaf

1 tablespoon salt

1 tablespoon coarsely cracked
    peppercorns

Put the chicken in a large pot with the onions, carrots, and celery. Pour on 4 quarts of water or enough to cover the ingredients by an inch or two. Bring to a boil and skim the foam that rises to the top. When the foam stops rising, add the parsley and bay leaf, salt, and peppercorns.

Partially cover the pot and simmer for about 1½ hours. Remove the chicken, testing to make sure it is done. Remove the meat from the bones and return the bones to the pot, continuing to simmer for an additional hour or two.

Strain the liquid through a cheesecloth-lined strainer and discard the solids. Let the stock cool, uncovered, before refrigerating. It will keep in the refrigerator for 2 or 3 days. Frozen, the stock will keep for several months.

# Beef Stock

Makes about 3 quarts

4 to 6 pounds meaty beef bones

2 onions, peeled and halved

3 carrots, scraped and
quartered

2 celery stalks, coarsely
chopped

6 to 8 parsley sprigs

1 teaspoon salt

1 teaspoon coarsely cracked
peppercorns

Preheat the oven to 450°F.

Roast the bones for 30 minutes, turning them once. Transfer them to a large pot.

Discard the fat from the roasting pan and deglaze the pan with 2 cups hot water. Add the contents of the pan to the pot along with the onions, carrots, celery, and 3 quarts cold water, or enough to cover the ingredients by an inch or two.

Bring to a boil, reduce to a simmer, and skim the foam that rises to the top. When the foam has stopped rising, add the parsley, salt, and pepper. Continue simmering for about 3 hours.

Strain the stock through a colander lined with several thicknesses of cheesecloth. Let the stock cool before refrigerating for up to 3 days. It will keep, frozen, for several months.

# Vegetable Stock

Makes about 3 quarts

2 large potatoes, quartered

3 carrots, peeled and coarsely
chopped

2 onions, peeled and coarsely
chopped

3 celery stalks (with leaves),
coarsely chopped

8 to 10 parsley sprigs

1 bay leaf

Salt

10 to 12 coarsely cracked
peppercorns

Combine all the ingredients in a large pot; add 3 quarts cold water.

Bring to a boil, lower the heat, and simmer, partially covered, for 1 hour.

Strain through a cheesecloth-lined colander. Let cool before refrigerating for 2 or 3 days. Frozen, the stock will keep for several months.

# Fish Stock

Makes about 2 quarts

2 onions, quartered

2 carrots, thickly sliced

2 celery stalks (with leaves),
coarsely sliced

10 black peppercorns, lightly
crushed

Several sprigs parsley, tied
together

4–5 pounds (or more) assorted
fish heads (remove the gills),
skeletons, and scraps from
white-fleshed fish

1 cup dry white wine

Combine all the ingredients in a stock pot, cover with 3 quarts of water. Bring to a boil, lower the heat, and simmer for 1 hour.

Let the stock cool before straining through a fine sieve lined with cheesecloth. Frozen, the stock will keep for several months; it will keep only a few days in the refrigerator.

# Metric Conversions

## Liquid Weights

| U.S. Measurements | Metric Equivalents |
|---|---|
| ¼ teaspoon | 1.23 ml |
| ½ teaspoon | 2.5 ml |
| ¾ teaspoon | 3.7 ml |
| 1 teaspoon | 5 ml |
| 1 dessertspoon | 10 ml |
| 1 tablespoon (3 teaspoons) | 15 ml |
| 2 tablespoons (1 ounce) | 30 ml |
| ¼ cup | 60 ml |
| ⅓ cup | 80 ml |
| ½ cup | 120 ml |
| ⅔ cup | 160 ml |
| ¾ cup | 180 ml |
| 1 cup (8 ounces) | 240 ml |
| 2 cups (1 pint) | 480 ml |
| 3 cups | 720 ml |
| 4 cups (1 quart) | 1 liter |
| 4 quarts (1 gallon) | 3¾ liters |

## Dry Weights

| U.S. Measurements | Metric Equivalents |
|---|---|
| ¼ ounce | 7 grams |
| ⅓ ounce | 10 grams |
| ½ ounce | 14 grams |
| 1 ounce | 28 grams |
| 1½ ounces | 42 grams |
| 1¾ ounces | 50 grams |
| 2 ounces | 57 grams |
| 3 ounces | 85 grams |
| 3½ ounces | 100 grams |
| 4 ounces (¼ pound) | 114 grams |
| 6 ounces | 170 grams |
| 8 ounces (½ pound) | 227 grams |
| 9 ounces | 250 grams |
| 16 ounces (1 pound) | 464 grams |

## Temperatures

| Fahrenheit | Celsius (Centigrade) |
|---|---|
| 32° F (water freezes) | 0° C |
| 200° F | 95° C |
| 212° F (water boils) | 100° C |
| 250° F | 120° C |
| 275° F | 135° C |
| 300° F (slow oven) | 150° C |
| 325° F | 160° C |
| 350° F (moderate oven) | 175° C |
| 375° F | 190° C |
| 400° F (hot oven) | 205° C |
| 425° F | 220° C |
| 450° F (very hot oven) | 230° C |
| 475° F | 245° C |
| 500° F (extremely hot oven) | 260° C |

## Length

| U.S. Measurements | Metric Equivalents |
|---|---|
| ⅛ inch | 3 mm |
| ¼ inch | 6 mm |
| ⅜ inch | 1 cm |
| ½ inch | 1.2 cm |
| ¾ inch | 2 cm |
| 1 inch | 2.5 cm |
| 1¼ inches | 3.1 cm |
| 1½ inches | 3.7 cm |
| 2 inches | 5 cm |
| 3 inches | 7.5 cm |
| 4 inches | 10 cm |
| 5 inches | 12.5 cm |

## Approximate Equivalents

1 kilo is slightly more than 2 pounds

1 liter is slightly more than 1 quart

1 meter is slightly over 3 feet

1 centimeter is approximately ⅜ inch

# Index